BURWAY BOOKS

CHURCH STRETTON

A Shropshire Town and its People

100M
200M
N
Halls
Close
Workhouse
Inclosure
Bank
ASHBROOK
Clay Pits
Nether Hill
Long Hills
Brooksbury and Clay Pits
Scotchmans
Piece
RECTORY
Matthews
Meadow
Broad
Meadow
London Meadow
Wet
Meadow
Priss
Hill
Brick Kiln
Meadow
Prosser Yard
Pool
Pool
Talbot
Field
Gate
Meadow
Green Me
WORLD'S
END
Horse Piece
Line
CHURCH STRETTON
THE PLAN AND FIELD NAMES ARE BASED ON THE
TITHE APPORTIONMENT AND MAP, c. 1840.

Church Stretton

A Shropshire Town and its People

David Bilbey

Phillimore

1985

Published by
PHILLIMORE & CO LTD
Shopwyke Hall, Chichester, Sussex

ISBN 0 85033 569 8

Printed and bound in Great Britain by
BILLING & SONS LTD
Worcester, England

For Jean

An unusual view of the church of St Laurence.

CONTENTS

The back of the *Buck's Head* which is shown as the Manor House on some maps. It is probably the building in which the Manor Courts were held.

LIST OF ILLUSTRATIONS

PREFACE AND ACKNOWLEDGEMENTS

It is said that when Paul Cezanne had finished painting a picture he would leave it wherever he had been working and go home . . . had it not been for his wife, who collected his masterpieces, many of them would have been lost forever, and the world would have been so much the poorer. It is, in fact, the 'doing', the 'creating', which is to me, and presumably was to Cezanne, the important part of the effort of writing or drawing, and that is why there is a certain sadness when a work is completed and the process of tying up the loose ends and writing out the list of acknowledgements etc. is underway. There is sadness too when one realises how much has had to be left out. Six months ago 5,000 words and the captions to 171 illustrations, say 14,000 words altogether, seemed so much until I realised that the 36 monthly articles in 'Focus' already make a total of some 30,000 words about Church Stretton and even that work is far from complete.

However, I have tried, within the limits of my brief, to offer the reader a precis of the material I have been accumulating over the past six years or so. Perhaps in the future I shall be able to expand and re-write the story in greater detail.

The content of this book is the result of continuous research but it would never have been possible to write it had I not had the co-operation of so many people, both in learning the technique of researching local history and in a more humble but equally important way, the offering of information. Sometimes this involved long conversations, sometimes it was a few words hurriedly exchanged as I passed someone in the street. While I have tried to mention everyone who has helped I am bound to have forgotten someone—to any such person, my deepest apologies.

And apologies are due also to people from the past who have contributed to the life of this community and who I have either forgotten or simply have been unable to find room for. I am thinking in particular of Preston Nunn who was curate from 1824 until his death in 1877. I feel sure that he was responsible for the work of the parish while the well-to-do rectors up at the great house took the credit and the majority of the stipend. But there are so many others . . . a glance at the 1841 census reminds one of John Faulkner, landlord of the *Crown*, James Heighway of the Free School, who was to enumerate the 1861 census, Eleanor Owen, a charwoman who lived in Back Lane, Martha Powell, a wool-picker, Mary Lewis, a laundress, John Belton, who had the farm next to the *Crown*, Thomas Gough, stonemason, Mary Wood, baker, Edward Marston, tailor, and so many more.

I should like to express my thanks to the following: Joyce Barnett, Muriel and Robert Bebbington, Harry Boulton, Pat and Peggy Boughey,

Tony Carr and his colleagues at the Local Studies Library, Ida Chilcott, Tony Crowe (wearing his several hats), Gordon Davies, Philla Davies, Joyce Gilkes, Hettie Dormer, Stan Edwards, Ros Ephraim, Justin Evans, Sarah Foulkes, Leslie Franklin, Katie Gaskell, Helen Giles, Elizabeth Gourdie, Don Gregory, Marion Halford, Edith Hall, Pauline Haycock, Brian Hazeldine, Reg Heiron, Ian Hyslop, Ethel Mann, Patrick Mann, Mary Marsden, Madge Moran, Jack Oliver, Bruce Osborne, Ormond Phillips, Mary Pilner, George Preece, Charles Ross-Murray, Percy Round, Nancy Smout, Martin Speight, Percy Tarbuck, Ray Tipton, Barrie Trinder, Malcolm Wanklyn, Rosaleen Wateley and Richard Wheatley. And to the following I extend my thanks for permission to reproduce material in their possession: Cambridge University Collection copyright reserved numbers 2 & 4; Church Stretton Women's Institute 8a & b, 63, 98, 102, 109, 110, 113 & 124; Mrs. K. W. Gaskell 83; Mrs. E. Hall 137 & 138; Ian Hyslop 123 & 130 and the photograph from which I drew 121; Tim Jones for the photograph from which I drew 73; Mrs. R. Leadbeater 106; Mrs. D. Redmond 145; Russell Mulford 120; St Dunstan's 136 & 139; Shropshire County Libraries 20, 22, 30, 46, 61, 64, 68, 75, 78, 85, 86, 88, 93, 114, 116, 118, 126, 127, 135 & 143; Miss A. E. Smout 76 and the photograph from which I drew 62. All other photographs have been taken by the author, and all the pictures, maps and plans were drawn by the author.

Finally I would like to record my thanks to my wife who has undertaken much of the routine work which is so important in a project such as this. Her comments have been invaluable and without her encouragement I doubt if the book would ever have been completed.

DAVID BILBEY

CHURCH STRETTON
February 1985

Introduction

'Charity vaunteth not itself, is not puffed up.' These qualities which St Paul ascribes to charity might also be applied to Church Stretton. Travellers must, always, have been conscious that they were approaching Leominster, Shrewsbury, Hereford, Ludlow or other Marcher towns, which proclaim their presence from afar. Church Stretton, however, is a shy place which hides itself away and the traveller has to enter the town before being aware of its presence. The church of St Laurence, Ludlow, proudly standing on high land above the River Teme, is visible for miles around, while St Laurence, Church Stretton, modestly fades into the landscape.

The church of St Laurence, showing the striking perpendicular work on the tower

I doubt if we shall ever know who did first settle here—the Celts, a Romano-British family, or a Saxon tribe, but the fact that the name Stretton or Stretune is a Saxon word does lend credence to the suggestion that it was they who first established their tun, that is their township or farmstead, in the Stretton valley.

The Church Stretton Gap is long and tapering, being barely half a mile wide where the town itself is situated. The valley floor is flat and the bordering hills rise abruptly because two parallel sets of faults have let down the rocks and formed a miniature rift valley. The Romans built their road from *Viroconium* to *Bravonium* (Wroxeter to Leintwardine) along the east side of the gap, and the A49 now follows the course of this road for much of its journey through the parish. It skirts the foot of Caer Caradoc on whose summit is an Iron Age camp, the presence of which, combined with a local field name 'Battlefield' has created a tradition that this was the place where Caractacus made his last stand against the Romans. While historians cannot agree on the actual location of this battle they are in agreement that it was not at Stretton.

The Saxons often settled in close proximity to, but not actually on, Roman roads, which would further advance the suggestion that Stretton is a Saxon foundation. If we try to imagine the landscape before the first people arrived we shall realise that the lower part of the Town Brook Valley would have been a convenient place for them to locate their home. The site could not be seen from the Roman road, it was sheltered from storms, had a stream running through, and there were ideal defensive positions close by. Stretching out into the main valley, and contrasting with surrounding areas of heavy boulder clay, was a fan of light, well-drained, easily cultivated soil. Beyond, on the valley floor, was wet marshy land covered with willow and alder. When the woodland was cleared and some drainage carried out, this must have

Caer Caradoc (459m.) dominates the eastern side of the Stretton Gap

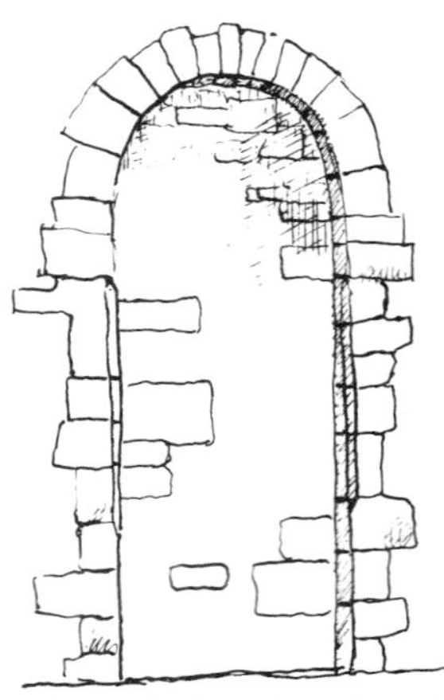

The walled-up interior of the north doorway of St Laurence's church

made excellent water meadows, producing the hay, so essential to the economy of the Middle Ages.

The first documentary account of Stretton is the Domesday records of 1086: *The earl himself holds Strtun. Earl Edwin held it with four berewicks. Here eight hides. In demesne are three ox teams. Six serfs and 18 villeins and eight boors with a priest have 12 teams. Here a mill and a church and in the wood five hayes. There might be six more teams. In the time of King Edward was worth £13. Now £5.* Lords of the manor were invariably absentee rulers and no great family has ever made its home here. At some time during the early 12th century the Normans rebuilt the church, but all that remains of this building are the walls of the nave, a walled-up north doorway and a south doorway which now leads into the vestry. In appearance this church was probably similar to Heath Chapel, in the Corve Dale, which still survives in its Romanesque form.

To the south of the town, dominating the Stretton Gap, is an impressive castle site standing on a gravel deposit which seems to be a terminal moraine, marking a halt in the northward retreat of the glacier at the end of the last Ice Age. This castle, called Brockhurst or Brocards, was first mentioned in 1155/56; it consisted of an inner bailey surrounded by a massive stone wall, a middle and possibly an outer bailey. There were also fishponds, a mill bank and a sluice crossing the valley and forming an access to the castle. However, by 1255 'there was regarded to be no castle at all and the men of Stretton stated that the fishponds had been drained and the fish sold'. Camden writing 350 years later said 'near Stretton in a valley are yet to be seen the rubbish of an old castle called Brocards castle and the same set amidst green meadows that before time were fishponds'.

All the evidence suggests that the end of the 12th and the beginning of the 13th centuries was a period of great change in Stretton. Alterations took place to the church, the east end being replaced by a central tower and transepts while a new transitional chancel was added. The supporting arches are also transitional, that is, they have both Norman and Early English characteristics, including the abaci which are square and moulded, while the arches are pointed. Similarly the carvings on the capitals exhibit features of both periods. The splendid trussed rafter roof of the nave may date from the 13th century. Just when the 'Sheila na gig' (a female fertility figure) was built into the north exterior wall of the nave is uncertain, and the weather has played havoc with her attributes so that she no longer compares with her sisters at Kilpeck or Holdgate. However, her presence reminds us that the Old Religion was intertwined in the spiritual beliefs of our ancestors throughout the Middle Ages. This was also a peak period in the plantation of medieval towns, and Stretton does exhibit many features which suggest that it was moved from Town Brook Valley to its present position at about that time. The skeletons of burgage plots, a wide market street, a back lane and what seems to be the remains of the 'aratral curve' of the open

Ornamental volutes on the heads of transitional columns supporting the tower of St Laurence's church

fields on which the town was built, can still be traced. On 26 June 1214 King John granted to Stretton a charter to hold a market on Wednesdays and a yearly fair on the Feast of the Assumption. This was changed when Edward III, in 1336, gave Stretton to the Earl of Arundel, and in the following year granted a weekly market on Thursdays and a yearly fair on the eve, the day and the morrow of the Exaltation of the Holy Cross. In 1309 a custom called *Passagium Carectarum,* that is toll on carts passing through the vill, produced 20 shillings, testifying to the growing importance of Stretton as a route town during the Middle Ages. In 1337 the name Chirchestretton was recorded for the first time.

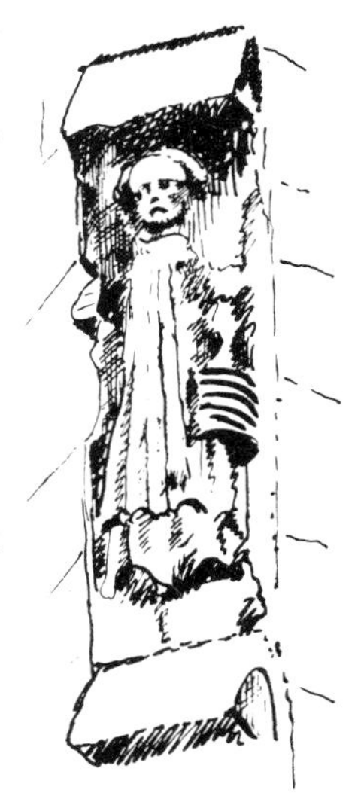

St Laurence, holding his gridiron, looks down on Church Stretton from the tower

D. H. S. Cranage, author of *An Architectural Account of the Churches of Shropshire*, feels that there could have been work carried out on the church during the 14th century when some windows may have been inserted. During the Perpendicular period considerable alterations and additions were carried out on the tower making it the most impressive feature of the building. While the rubble stonework of the transitional walls appears for some distance above the church roof, the whole of the upper part is Perpendicular with rich and effective ornamentation. The stonework here is well-finished ashlar, the windows are cusped and pointed under square heads, while the gargoyles, now unfortunately considerably decayed, are still unusually fine and grotesque. Attached to the south-east buttress is a figure of St Laurence, the patron saint, holding his gridiron. At the time of the Reformation the dark candle-lit interior of the medieval church was transformed and the focus of worship moved from the altar to the pulpit. The great rood, the rood-beam and the screen were dispensed with, the stained glass was removed from the windows, statues were destroyed, while any wall paintings disappeared under layers of whitewash. As time went by box pews and fine Jacobean woodwork were added, so that until the Gothic revivalists of the 19th century had their way the townspeople worshipped in a Prayer Book church.

Like most towns built of timber and thatch Church Stretton suffered a great fire. In the fire of 1593 the church was untouched, but the damage to other buildings was so severe that a collection was made in aid of the sufferers, by order of the Council in the Marches and Wales, the money being received by William Posterne on behalf of himself and his fellow townsmen whose houses and goods had been burnt. The rebuilding was in timber-frame, some of which still hides beneath Georgian and Victorian exteriors. The *King's Arms* and Tudor Cottage date from that time. The inn has a fine close-studded north wall and interesting interior woodwork, while stucco on the front conceals more timber framing. Tudor Cottage is unique in that it has two hewn or false jetties, a rare feature indeed. The jetty or overhang, a term used for the outward protrusion of the top storey over the one below, in timber-framed buildings is a feature of the 15th and 16th centuries. The origin of the jettied construction is not known; it may have evolved to provide extra space on upper floors or to overcome structural

A view of the King's Arms *as it might have looked when it was first built*

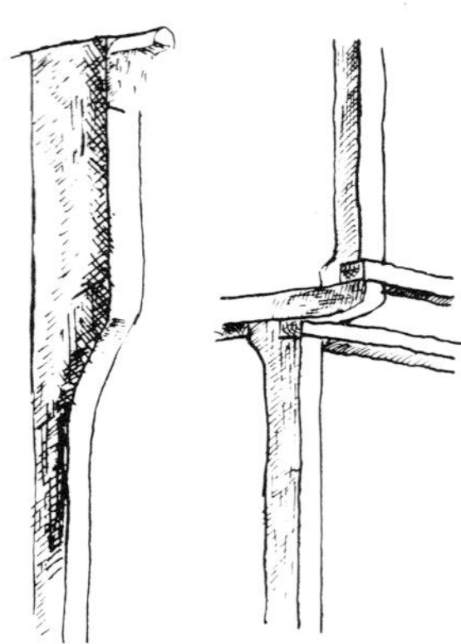

Hewn or false jetties compared with the traditional method of jetty construction

problems, or it may simply have been a status symbol—after all, jetties are far more common on the street side of houses than at their rears. In the hewn or false jetty, as in Tudor Cottage, the corner timbers have been cut away to give the appearance of a jettied construction, and if a householder was willing to go to such lengths to produce this effect, then the idea of the jetty as a status symbol becomes more plausible. Originally the cross-wing of the house extended to the rear, but it seems to have been altered in 1779.

In 1617 Bonham Norton, King's Printer and lord of the manor, who was married to Jane Owen of Condover, provided the money to erect a market hall in the wide market street. It was a splendid timber-framed structure similar to other market halls in the area and there have been claims that it was framed by the legendary John Abel, though there is no documentary evidence to support this suggestion. It was finally pulled down in 1839 to be replaced a year later by an edifice, described by Pevsner as 'in a 17th century style with Tuscan columns and arches above'. This in its turn was demolished as unsafe.

Despite considerable research we have found very few references to Church Stretton during the 17th century. The town was never a corporate borough so there are few records. The civil war seems to have passed it by, possibly because no local landowning family dragged its servants and tenants to war on one side or the other.

The physical presence of the Long Mynd (517m. at its highest point) has exerted its influence over Stretton ever since people settled in the valley. During the Middle Ages the lord of the manor, the Earl of Arundel, had occasion to write to his steward to inform him that the owners of animals from various townships with common rights on the Long Mynd must mark or brand their stock or risk confiscation. For almost 300 years there have been disputes over common rights, and in 1610 the Church Stretton riots involved townspeople and farmers. The commoners have always acted with vigour in defence of their rights, and in more recent times the local council took it upon itself to fence a triangle of common land by the Old Rectory wall—next morning the fencing had been removed and lay in a tidy pile awaiting collection. The last fair of the year was called 'Dead Man's Fair' because, it is said, people had died crossing the Long Mynd when returning to their homes in bad weather. In January 1865 the Rev. Donald Carr, vicar of Woolstaston, was lost in a blizzard when returning from Ratlinghope. Blinded by snow and without boots, stick or hat he was eventually guided to a house in the Carding Mill valley by children's voices. His account, *A night in the snow*, has been reprinted.

St Margaret's, Ratlinghope, where Rev. Carr preached in 1865

As time went by, timber-framed buildings were replaced by Georgian houses; others were disguised under a skin of brick or stucco. Interiors suffered in the same way, plaster laths being nailed to oak ceiling beams while timber on walls was hacked to provide a key for plaster. One of the earliest buildings erected in the new style was No. 17 High Street, previously known as Berry's Messuage. Here the builder had to place an early 18th-century town house on a narrow burgage plot, as a result of which an excellent doorway with a fine cornice, big consoles and a typical fanlight, is sited on the side of the house down a narrow lane. The door opens on to an attractive hall and staircase leading to panelled first-floor rooms.

'Berry's Messuage', now No. 17 High Street—a rather fine Queen Anne house

Since the Middle Ages the gradual colonisation of the wide main street by buildings had left the town with a very small market place, and as a result the various livestock fairs spread out into other parts of the town. A photograph has been included showing the whole of Brook Street (Burway Road) taken over by a sheep market. Higher up the Burway and down Church Street was the area where pony fairs were held twice a year. These ponies came from the Long Mynd where, as a result of inbreeding, the stock had become so poor that Welsh stallions were introduced in an attempt to improve it. The effort came too late because, with the mechanisation of the underground workings in coal mines, the demand for ponies gradually died out. The ponies' hooves had kept the hills free of bracken, allowing grass to grow, not only for themselves, but for the sheep as well. Their absence has encouraged a rapid spread of bracken over the common land.

So far, our story has been concerned with Church Stretton as a collection of buildings. People have remained shadows in the background; we know of their existence, they were fined at the manor courts, they bought and sold property, they were born, married and died, often being buried in woollen, but from 1840 onwards a combination of census returns and tithe apportionment records allows us to identify individuals, find out where they lived, the work they carried out and to discover something about their families.

The 1841 census tells us that High Street was called the Bristol Road, and I would suggest that, in imagination, we leave Shropshire for a short while and stand on the motorway service area at Aust on the M4 to consider transport and communications in Church Stretton. A few miles away on the Welsh side of the Severn estuary the Romans built Caerwent on a road system linked to our Watling Street, while under the tidal race some seven kilometers downstream is the Severn railway tunnel, the opening of which transformed the local railway line, which Mr. Brassey had built between Shrewsbury and Hereford in 1852, into a major trunk route with its roots in the West Country and its branches in the North of England and Scotland. For many years before the opening of the Severn Bridge the Aust crossing was the site of an important ferry and an integral link in the Bristol-Chester Road of which the turnpike through the Strettons was a part. It was an important coaching route, but by 1840 this coaching-trade was already in decline as a result of the expansion of the railways. However, the northbound 'Royal Mail' from Hereford to Shrewsbury still left the *Talbot* at 4.30 each afternoon, and William Haverkam, the landlord, was described as 'Postmaster', a position which carried the responsibility of providing a free house-to-house

A milestone on High Street, the Bristol-Chester Road

The Hotel's *origins as the* Crown *are commemorated in the portico over the entrance to the bars*

delivery of letters. The *Talbot,* a Georgian-fronted building with extensive yards and stabling, situated at the southern entrance of the town, was still Stretton's superior inn, but 10 years later with the railway almost completed, it had been divided into two households, while the *Crown,* the nearest inn to the station, had become the most important hostelry. Within 15 years its name had been changed to the *Hotel* and considerable extensions had been built in a somewhat pixilated Victorian Gothic style. To achieve the necessary space a 16th-century malthouse had to be pulled down, but one stone was retained and incorporated in the wall of the new building. It reads 'erected by Copper & W his sonne ano dni 1587'. When the town expanded at the end of the century the *Hotel* was further extended and it remained the principal hotel in Church Stretton until the disastrous fire in 1968, when a member of staff and three children died. It never reopened as a hotel, but the name carries on in the old *Crown* premises where the porch over the doorway and the capitals to the columns which support it are modelled in the form of a crown.

Throughout its history Church Stretton has been a route town which offered services to the surrounding area. The weekly markets have flourished while fairs became increasingly important for the sale of livestock. It is as a service town that Stretton has continued to prosper; the *Talbot* was acquired by Samuel Bakewell, who converted it into a private lunatic asylum for gentlemen, while a hydropathic establishment (now the *Long Mynd Hotel*) was opened in 1900. However, the town has been most successful as a small holiday resort and more recently as a place of retirement and a home for commuters willing to travel long distances in order to live in pleasant surroundings.

There was little change in the plan of the town from Tudor times until the 20th century. An analysis of the census returns of the 19th century reveals a constant movement of population and shows that a majority of the heads of households and their wives were not born in Church Stretton. In 1676 the population of the parish, according to the religious census, was 431 people over the age of 16, one papist and two nonconformists. In 1841 the population of the township of Church Stretton was 631, plus three travelling chimney sweeps who, on the preceding night, slept in a barn. During the 19th century the church did not escape the enthusiasm of Victorian restorers. They removed the plaster and whitewash which had accumulated on the walls since the Reformation and in doing so not only erased the 10 commandments, creed, Lord's Prayer and texts, but probably destroyed the remains of any medieval wall paintings as well. Western aisles were added to the transepts, an organ loft to the north side of the chancel and a porch to the south doorway. This subsequently became a vestry when a new doorway was opened in the west wall of the nave. Furnishings did not escape the fervour of the restorers and the gallery, box pews, coat of arms and a carved Jacobean pulpit were removed.

The Hydropathic Establishment, now the Long Mynd Hotel

The latter was replaced by a typical Victorian pulpit. The oak screen which was erected has recently been removed, but perhaps we have learnt something from the past because it has been preserved as part of a new chapel in the north transept. The medieval screen, the great rood, stained glass, box pews and other treasures of the past just disappeared. Some church woodwork became part of the bar front of the *Raven*. A congregational chapel, designed by Joseph Bratton of Birkenhead, was opened in 1866. Eight years earlier, services were held under the market hall and as the weather worsened a room which had once been a carpenter's shop was procured. It was approached by a narrow ladder and not more than two-thirds of the congregation could stand upright.

This Victorian pulpit replaced a carved Jacobean one

During the mid-19th century there were five malthouses and the Beddoes' skinner's yard in the vicinity of the crossroads by the *Hotel*. Further up the hill was the rectory, the largest house in the area, with its extensive pleasure grounds and gardens spreading out into the Town Brook Valley and on to the nearby hillsides. The rectors of the period, Coleman, Pemberton, Owen Wilson and Noel Hill, were men of property. Pemberton let the rectory and moved into his newly-built home, Millichope Park in the Corvedale, in 1841. There seems little doubt that the first Bank House was a larger timber-frame building with extensive barns, coach-houses and outbuildings, occupied in 1838 by John Broome who farmed the largest acreage in the township. It was probably already in a poor state of repair, and in the 1890s was replaced by the present neo-timber-framed structure.

Until the public elementary endowed school was opened in 1861, Burway House was the free school. It was erected in 1779 on the site of an older school supposed to have been built on waste land. The encroachments were confirmed by the commissioners in an Act of Parliament in 1787/88 for enclosing commons and waste land in the manor of Church Stretton, and land was allocated to provide £27 per annum towards a schoolmaster's salary which amounted to £40, plus a free house. In 1841 James Heighway was probably the schoolmaster, but 10 years later he was a general grocer in Bristol Road, while in 1861 he was an accountant and enumerator of the census. His successor at Burway House was Thomas Cureton who subsequently moved to the new school.

During the mid-19th century there were two doctors. One was William Wilding, who, about 1838, moved from a Georgian house at the top of Lake Lane, later occupied by George Preece, and pulled down in the 1920s to make way for Lloyd's bank, to No. 17 High Street. This house seems to have been occupied by surgeons for over 100 years. His son, Richard, and grandson, William, followed him in the practice, and the family lived there until the 1890s when the house was sold and became a private hotel. The other doctor was Charles Mott who owned what is now Insurance House, and after his death the practice was carried on by the McClintocks. Next door to

Dr. Mott's house in High Street

This wheelpit still exists in the old metal working area behind Salt's

the Wildings was the *Lion Inn,* and Jonathan Mills, the landlord, also rented Lion Meadow to the rear. As the increasing traffic of the 20th century drove the livestock sales off the streets this became 'sheep sales field', remaining so until the King's Court complex was built there, thus breaking one of the few remaining links with King John's charter.

In 1840, No. 19 High Street was occupied by Thomas Glover, a shopkeeper, and Thomas Gough, a stonemason, had his workship in one of the buildings which extend down the burgage plot. Also at the rear, in 1841, was the Childe's workshops: they were tinmen and subsequently the area was the workplace of a blacksmith and a wheelwright. The wheelpit and the last of the blacksmith's shops, no longer used, still exist. Glover's shop was taken over by Henry Wood and became a substantial ironmongers, while part of the frontage was, for a time, the Shrewsbury Old Bank—open Thursdays and fair days. Eventually the premises were acquired by Henry Salt, who built the superb Victorian frontage in 1901. Priestleys at No. 1 The Square, was the *Plough Inn* until January 1948, when the licence was transferred to the *Sandford Hotel*; it was expected that the opening of the bypass would cause trade to move away from the town. Next door, No. 2, has an interesting frontage and a good chimney stack. It seems to have been squeezed into the corner and my hypothesis is that Russell's, the house and office of John Russell, estate agent, represents the old medieval building line and that the *Plough,* the market hall and buildings to the south colonised the wide street, forming a narrow lane which in its turn was also filled in. In 1841 John Craig, a maltster, occupied No. 3, but he had left the district within 10 years and the McCartneys, travelling tea dealers from Scotland, lived there for a time. They took over the malting trade which they seem to have rationalised when they built the splendid malthouse in Sandford Avenue. The *Raven* was an inn until quite recently and further south is the *Buck's Head* where the end wall of the cross wing, with its diapers in vitrified blue brick, stone dressings and quoins, bears a striking resemblance to Plaish Hall, *c.* 1540, where the use of brick is reputedly the earliest in the county. On older O.S. plans the *Buck's Head* is referred to as the Manor House, a title for which we have found no documentary evidence. However, the manor courts were probably held there, although the records of the period 1720–60 state, time and time again, that the court was held 'in the usual place'. The inn yard was across the road where a 16th-century, three-bay, timber-framed barn was disintegrating until it was beautifully restored by Lt.-Col. and Mrs. Witting. Jubilee buildings are an interesting example of the use of Ruabon brick, while behind is a court of much older cottages. William Marston, a tailor, and Samuel Morgan, a shopkeeper, lived there, but the latter moved his large household to the shop on the corner which is now Crocker's. Next door was the *Britannia Inn*, under the eaves of which are a row of iron rings. The only explanation we can find for them is that they were for balancing the long poles used for dragging

The eastern front of the Buck's Head

burning thatch from roofs. There was a poor house which became redundant when the grim stone Union Workhouse was erected on the Shrewsbury turnpike; the latter was itself demolished to make way for the new school. All that survives is a part of the infirmary which is incorporated in the swimming baths. The almshouses, lock-up and numerous cottages were pulled down so that the Silvester Horne Institute could be built in 1916. Opposite is a narrow lane dividing what used to be the *Queen's Head* from the garden of Greengates. Here there used to be two small timber-framed cottages in one of which the Haughtons lived—they were beastleaches, who would have done simple medical work, such as pulling teeth and helping with the healing of animals. In *Precious Bane*, Mary Webb says, 'in one corner [of the market place] the beastleach was pulling teeth at a penny each and had a crowd watching'. During 1871, in a room over the stables of the *Queen's Head,* lived an agricultural labourer, his wife, mother-in-law, and eight children.

'Crocker's' has been owned by many shopkeepers since Samuel Morgan took it over in about 1840

In 1841 Ragleth House was a girls' boarding school. Ann Corfield, the principal, and her three sisters taught 32 girls between the ages of seven and 14; the alterations which have spoilt the Georgian front were probably undertaken about this time. The house is more commonly remembered as Dr. Gooch's surgery. By 1861 the Corfield sisters had retired and Susannah Shingles had opened a day and boarding school for girls at the Park in Cub Lane—now Park House in Church Way.

As the 19th century advanced, Church Stretton's reputation as a holiday resort increased. In the autumn of 1884 the Rev. Holland Sandford, rector of the neighbouring parish of Eaton-under-Heywood, and one of the Sandfords of the Isle, called a meeting of local men of influence and formed a committee to aid him in planting an avenue of lime trees in Station Road. The beauties of the Quarry in Shrewsbury and of many great European cities were quoted as examples, and after numerous meetings and much argument the first trees were planted at a ceremony on 19 December 1884. Subsequently the avenue was extended along the New Hazler Road to the Hazler turnpike. It should be pointed out that two members of the rector's committee were Ralph Benson, the largest landowner in the district, and Riou Benson, his uncle, and that a fortnight before the first meeting the breakthrough had been made in the Severn railway tunnel, an event which I have already suggested was to turn the Shrewsbury–Hereford line into a trunk route. Whether the Bensons saw this as a means of developing the town and so increasing land values, we shall never know. A few days after the trees were planted a number were slashed and despite the offer of comparatively large rewards the offenders were never found; in such a small community they must have been known so one can only surmise that people whose lives often terminated in the workhouse had little sympathy for the planting of lime trees and the creation of Sandford Avenue. Early in 1885 another committee was established

The only part of the Union Workhouse to have survived

A corner of the New Bank House, a good example of the neo-timber-frame building which is a hallmark of Church Stretton

with the object of 'further improving the approaches to the town of Church Stretton'.

During the next two decades the Stretton Land Company and the Stretton Building Company were established; they built roads on the surrounding hills—Trevor Hill, Clive Avenue, Cunnery Road, Kenyon Road, etc., and sold building plots which varied considerably in status. Their efforts were only partly successful, and some of the roads were never completed, but, despite this, although some empty plots remained, a number of impressive houses were erected. 'This was the time', as Pevsner so aptly puts it, 'of the great fashion for neo-half-timbering', and as he concludes 'half-timber is the hallmark of Church Stretton'. The first houses in this style were a terrace in Church Street dated 1885, followed by Barry Parker's Woodcote, the Rowans, Arden House, Bank House, and numerous other residences which make the town unique. This was also the period when the town aspired to become a spa and the Hydropathic Establishment had been completed by 1900. Unfortunately, hydrotherapy was in decline and it must be remembered that there was no spa water in the valley, only pure spring water which was being exploited by the Stretton Hills Mineral Water Company at Cwm Dale and the Church Stretton Aerated Water Company in the Carding Mill Valley. The nearest spa water was at Wentnor on the western side of the Long Mynd and a scheme to pipe it to Stretton and to build a pump room came to nought, as did a projected funicular railway, similar to the one at Bridgnorth. The Hydro (now the *Long Mynd Hotel*) actually used water brought by train from Llandrindod Wells. Church Stretton continued to function as a small market town and a holiday resort, but increasing traffic in the late 1930s began to clog the High Street and a bypass was built, approximately on the site of the Roman road. It was almost complete in 1939 at the outbreak of war, when it was taken over as a vehicle park by the army. St Dunstan's moved from their vulnerable premises at Ovingdean, in Sussex, taking over the *Long Mynd Hotel,* Brockhurst and other premises for the duration of the war.

The ruined weigh-bridge office in the station yard

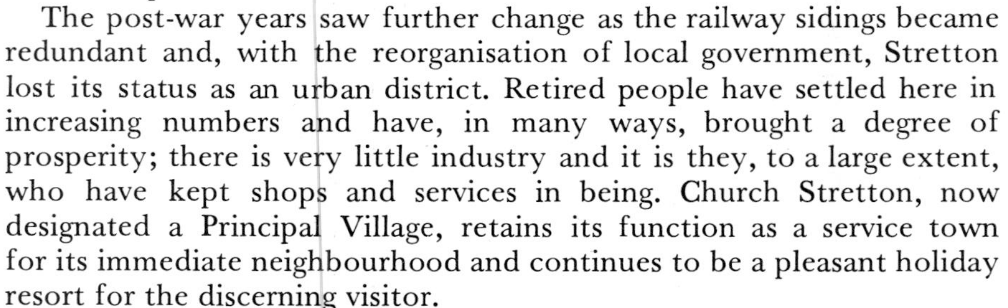

The post-war years saw further change as the railway sidings became redundant and, with the reorganisation of local government, Stretton lost its status as an urban district. Retired people have settled here in increasing numbers and have, in many ways, brought a degree of prosperity; there is very little industry and it is they, to a large extent, who have kept shops and services in being. Church Stretton, now designated a Principal Village, retains its function as a service town for its immediate neighbourhood and continues to be a pleasant holiday resort for the discerning visitor.

The Plates

The Crown *became the* Hotel *in 1865. Pevsner describes it as debased Victorian, but many feel that this main entrance is a fine example of Gothic revival.*

Brockhurst Castle stripped of trees to show the inner and outer bailey. The roots of mature trees, aided by sheep, are rapidly eroding the site.

In the Beginning

EY

The Long Mynd
Church Stretton
All Stretton
Little Stretton
Ashlet
Caer Caradoc Hill
Hill Fort
Helmeth Hill
Hazler Hill
Ragleth Hill

Roman Road
Bypass
Cwm Dale
'Pop' works
Union Workhouse
Ashbrook
Carding Mill Valley
Swimming Pool
Motts Road
The Burway
To Pole Cottage
Town Brook Valley
The Hydro
The council houses
Brockhurst Castle
Battlefield
Dennis Williams's farm
Railway houses

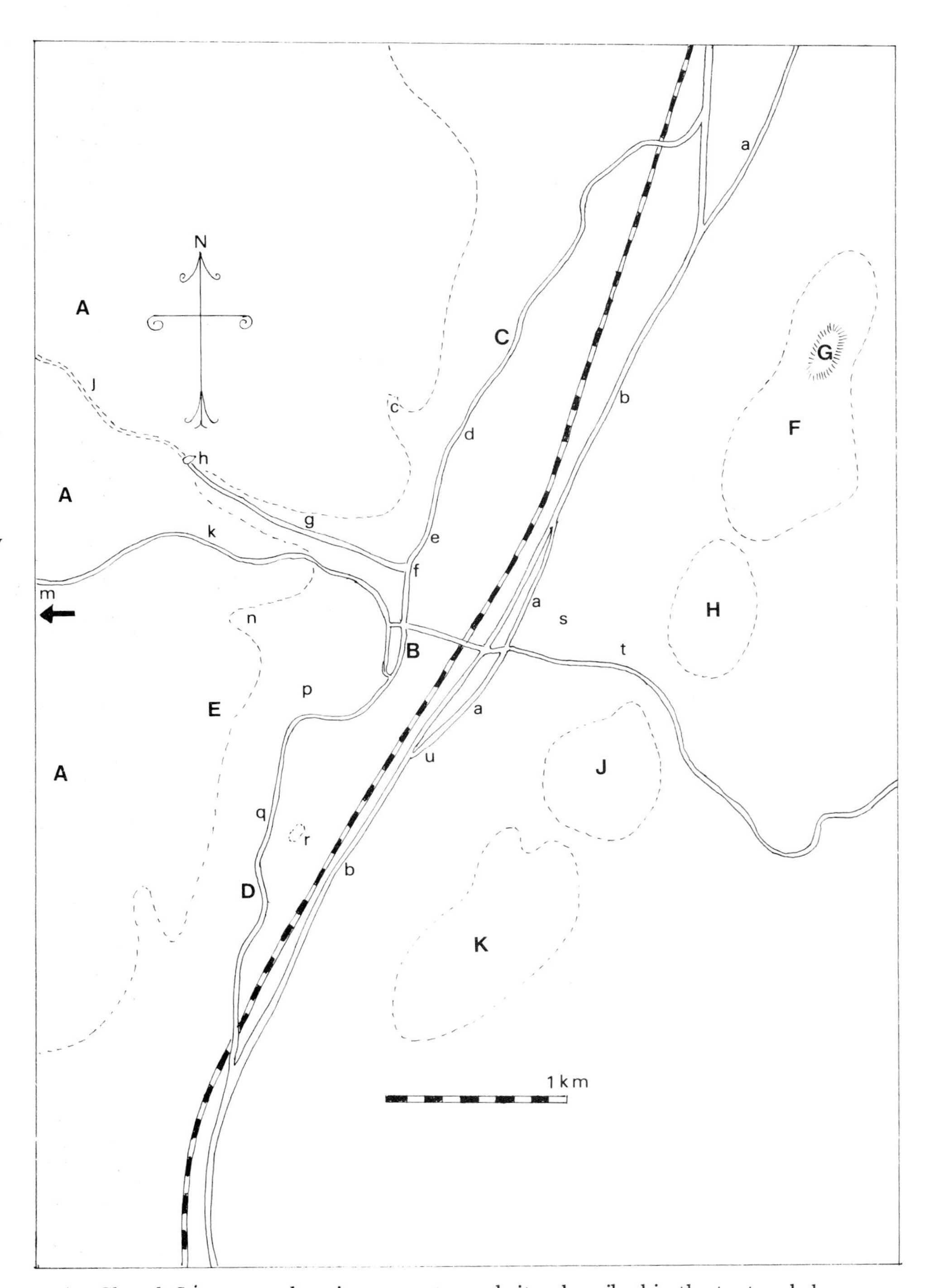

1. Church Stretton and environs—routes and sites described in the text and shown in the illustrations.

2. Aerial view of the Stretton Hills from the north which vividly emphasises the importance of the Stretton Gap. The Roman road stands out very clearly.

3. Looking north from the slopes of Ashlet the narrowness of the gap, in the vicinity of Church Stretton, is obvious. The medieval settlement is hidden behind the woods in the middle distance but the development of the town during the 20th century is shown spreading over the valley floor and on to the slopes of the hills.

4. (*above*) Despite its uncomfortable and exposed position on the summit of Caer Caradoc, the hill fort contains numerous hut platforms and there can be little doubt that it was a permanent settlement. It had an inturned entrance, guard rooms and the approach was by an engineered path cut in the hillside.

5. (*right*) This photograph, taken to the south of Church Stretton and approximately opposite Brockhurst, shows how the Roman road had, by the early 20th century, become little more than a field path.

10. North doorways, the Devil's doors, were supposed to have been left open during baptismal services for the escape of exorcised evil. On the other hand, medieval worship involved processions around the church for which such doorways must have been used. Or perhaps they were entrances on the side of the church nearest the local settlement.

11. Historians agree that there were major alterations to the church of St Laurence about A.D. 1200 when the Norman chancel was pulled down and a crossing, transepts and a new chancel were built. The transitional arches which supported the new tower remain 'in situ', while its stonework can be seen from the outside of the building.

12. (*right*) 'The abaci are square and moulded in the usual Norman manner and the capitals have ornamental volutes' (Cranage). Other transitional features can be clearly seen in the photograph.

13. (*below*) The crossing is one of the finest features of the interior of the church. The central tower is supported by four arches which reveal a mixture of Norman and Early English work. The abaci are Norman but the arches are pointed in the Early English style.

14. One of the lancet windows which has survived. Th one is in the north transept. It is important to try to imagine how dark the church must have been when all the windows were of this size and what must have been the effect of flickering candles lighting up the brilliant colours of the wall paintings.

15. The Perpendicular tower is undoubtedly the best exterior feature of the church. The gargoyles are unfortunately considerably decayed but are still unusually fine and grotesque.

16. Sheila-na-gig is a technical term for fertility figures on churches in the British Isles and also on castles in Ireland. It seems that they were bound up with fertility rites and that they were perfectly acceptable until the Church decided to wipe out the 'Old Religion' late in the 15th century.

17. There are hundreds of these fertility figures in Europe and it is safe to assume that there were many more in this country before the despoilers of the Reformation and the restorers of the 19th century had their way. They were not intended to be obscene. These Sheila-na-gigs are from Kilpeck in Herefordshire, and Holdgate and Abdon in the Corvedale.

The Reformation and After

18. Benefaction board in the church: 'Thomas Hawkes Gent. 1708 Left a piece of land, being part of Little Stretton Pools, the rents thereof to be distributed yearly among the poor of this Parish.' He also left 'a Messuage or Tenement situated in this town called Walter's House.'. 'Four alms houses adjoining Walter's House' were erected in 1820.

19. Bellringers Instructions (1773):
If that to ring you do come here
You must ring well with hand and ear
And if a bell you overthrow
4d to pay before you go
And if you ring with spur or hat
6d you must pay for that
Or if in this place you swear or curse
12d to pay pull out your purse.

20. A drawing of St Laurence's church made in 1841 before the pyramidal roof had been added to the tower or the western aisles to the transepts. The artist unwittingly reveals, by his drawing of the dormer windows on Nos. 43 and 45 Church Street, that their roofs have been raised since then.

21. No doubt there was a screen here in medieval times which would have been removed at the Reformation. The Victorians, in their desire to return to what they imagined a true Gothic interior to have been, added this screen but in 1984 it was decided that it must be taken down. It was incorporated in the new Emmaus chapel.

22. This memorial representing the gridiron on which St Laurence died, with simulated flames of twisted copper, was erected to the memory of three boys, visitors to the *Hotel*, who lost their lives when it was burned down in 1968.

23. The Church Hall can hardly be described as exceptional architecture but it is representative of a significant period of building, particularly in country areas, when earlier in this century village and memorial halls were erected in corrugated iron. Many have been replaced by modern buildings. The Church Stretton hall has, in addition, a neo-timber-frame gable.

The Churchyard

24. Churchyard crosses were usually surmounted by elaborate crucifixes which were destroyed afte the Reformation and occasionally replaced by a sundial. This stonework bears the initials 'TW & IW' who were churchwardens in 1713. On the top is a brass dial covering an earlier one with the inscription 'LAT 52 28' and 'The Vernon Ludlow'. The gnomon is missing.

25. The gravestone of Margreat Morgan: *Here lyeth ye Body of Margreat Morgan who dyd March 2 Anno dom 1701 aged 74.* Charles I had been on the throne for two years when she was born (1627). She lived through the Civil War, Interregnum, the Restoration and the Glorious Revolution. Queen Anne was crowned the year after she died.

26. The Thursday Grave:
Ann wife of Thomas Cook.
On a Thursday she was born
On a Thursday made a bride
On a Thursday her leg was broke
and on a Thursday died.

27. The Edwards Memorial. This stone has been included as an example of pleasant calligraphy and for the interesting spelling of 'daughter' at the bottom. One can only assume that the stonemason was not sure how to spell the word and adopted this novel solution!

31. Two branches of the Hyslop family moved into Stretton during the 19th century and William took over Bakewell's lunatic asylum *c.* 1865. When he died in 1883 his eldest son, Captain, later Lieutenant Colonel, Campbell Hyslop, the builder of 'Woodcote', succeeded him. The latter was an enthusiastic officer of the Volunteers; he died on a home defence posting in 1915.

32. Charles Silvester Horne (1865-1914) was a renowned Congregational preacher, Liberal M.P. for Ipswich and builder of the White House, Sandford Avenue, as a holiday retreat to which he eventually moved. He died on a lecture tour of the U.S. and Canada and his body was brought back to Church Stretton. The Institute named after him was financed by public subscription.

More Modern Churches

33. The west front of the Congregational, now the United Reformed church designed by Joseph Bratton of Birkenhead and opened for services in 1866. It was renovated in 1886, a manse was built in 1909 and the church was refurbished in 1937. The church hall was added in 1957.

34. (*above*) The Methodist church was erected in 1906 on building plots sold by the Stretton Land Company, which was developing the Crossways area of the town. It is a typical building of its period in which Ruabon brick has been used to good effect.

35. (*left*) The Roman Catholic church is dedicated to the Saxon St Milburga. It was built in 1929; previously the congregation had worshipped at the Ross family's home in Watling Street and later at Manchester House in Churchway (known as Cub Lane on older maps).

The Middle Ages—A Planned Town

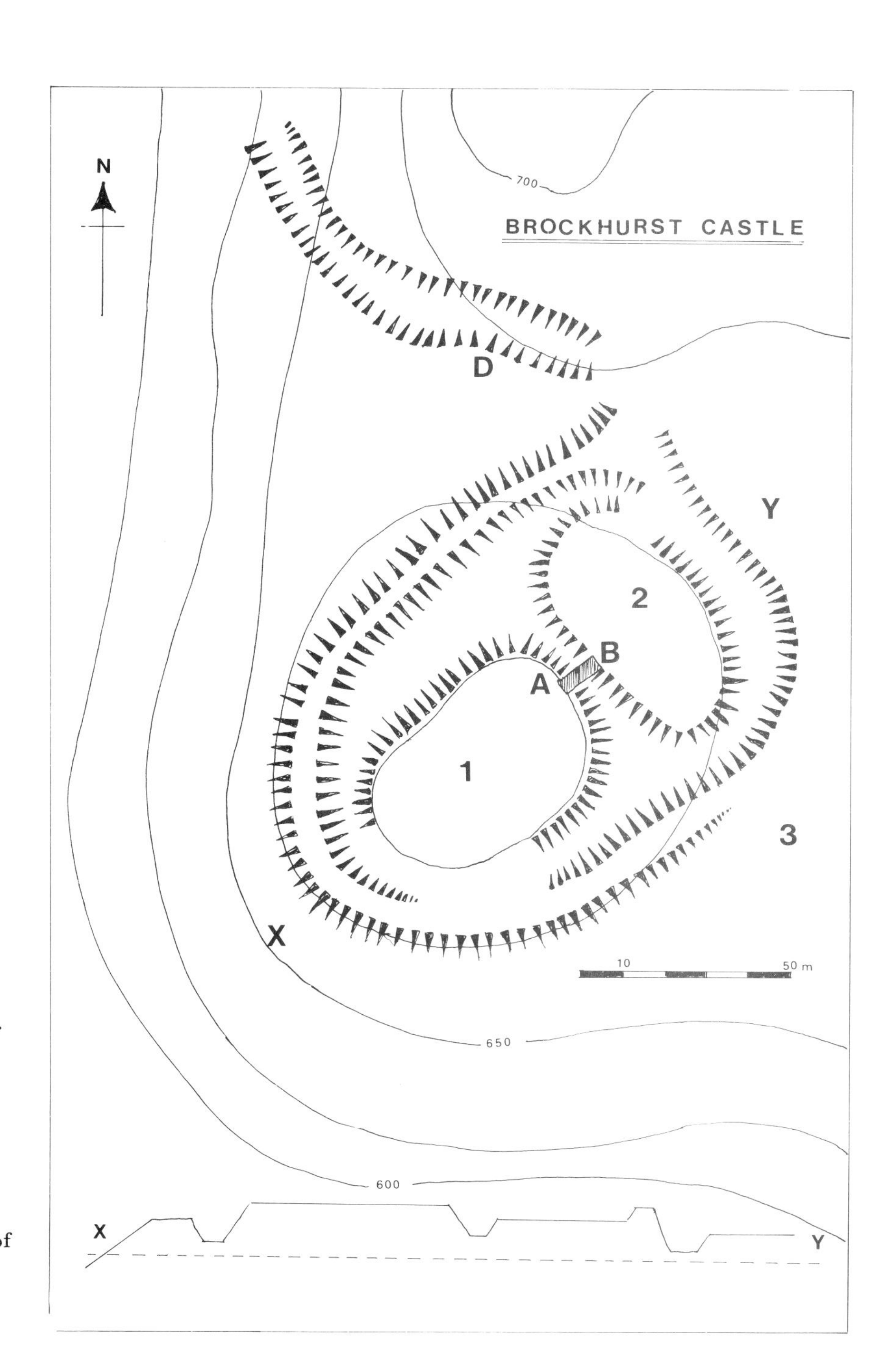

36. Plan of Brockhurst Castle.

KEY

1. Inner Bailey
2. Middle Bailey
3. Outer Bailey

A. Traces of wall
B. Slight causeway
C. Rubble and sharp angle of slope
D. End of terrace way
XY. Section across site

37. Brockhurst Castle from Ashlet. The inner and middle baileys are completely hidden by trees whose roots, combined with the activities of sheep, are rapidly eroding the site. The causeway is just visible. To the right are Camden's 'green meadows which before time were fishponds'. Beyond, under Ragleth, is the Roman road (A49) and Mr. Brassey's Shrewsbury-Hereford railway.

38. Plan of Stretton at the close of the Middle Ages (conject-
This attempts to show how the original wide main street was
croached upon by various buildings, solidified market stalls as
they have been called, which eventually formed a new west si
of the High Street or Bristol Road.

39. The right for a market to be held on Wednesdays was first granted by King John in 1214, while Edward III's charter allowed for a market on Thursdays. In 1616 James I granted the right to hold a market on Thursdays to Bonham Norton who was lord of the manor at that time. Market day is still Thursday today. This drawing shows market day in 1984.

40. (*above*) In the foreground of this drawing is Lion Meadow or Sheep Sales Field, as it was called until its disappearance beneath the buildings of Kin Court, recently-built apartments occupied, in the main, by retired people. Beyond are burgage plots at the rear of buildings on High Street.

41. (*left*) Church Street was referred to as Back La in all the Manor Court records of the 18th century. The census returns of 1881 use the name, as did ma older people until quite recently. Since the mid-19t century it has been gradually colonised by buildings

42. Looking south from the church tower. The backs of buildings in High Street are on the left of this picture, while Back Lane is on the right. In between are long narrow burgage plots, many now encroached upon by buildings of various types.

43. Only the small market place remains to show the width of the original medieval High Street. Buildings fronting on to it are of various periods but the pattern of burgage plots which have been encroached upon is again quite clearly visible.

44. Plan of the town *c.* 1838 based on the Tithe Apportionment and Map.

KEY

A. Bristol Road or High Street
B. Back Lane, now Church Street
C. Shrewsbury Turnpike
D. Brook Street, now Burway Road
E. Cub Lane, now Churchway
F. Lake Lane, subsequently Station Road and now Sandford Avenue
G. Town Brook
H. The Free School
J. The *Crown*
K. Copper's malthouse
L. The Market Hall
M. Berry's Messuage—No. 17
N. The church of St Laurence
P. Lion Meadow
Q. Bright's Messuage
R. The Old Barn
S. Walter's House—the Poor House
T. The Misses Corfield's Boarding School for Girls
U. Tudor Cottage
V. The Talbot complex, later Stretton House—Lunatic Asylum for gentlemen
W. Site of the Public Elementary Endowed School
X. Talbot Meadow
Y. The additional burial ground
Z. Nos. 29/37 Church Street

a. Bank House
b. Spring Cottage
c. Beddoes' Skin yard
d. Site of the Posting Establishment
e. George Windsor's Post Office
f. George Preece's house
g. The home of Elijah Price, the weaver
h. Site of Thos. Rich's shop
j. Site of the Malthouse
k. Harry Boulton's
l. The *Lion*
m. The *Plough*
n. John Craig, maltster, then the McCartneys, travelling tea dealers
o. Proffit's
p. Woods', ironmongers, subsequently Salt's
q. The Childe's workshop
r. The *Buck's Head*
s. Church gates
t. The Fewtrell's cottage
u. Sam Morgan's shop
v. Dr. Charles Mott's house
w. The *King's Arms*
x. Site of the *Brittania*
y. Greengates
z. The Houghton's (beastleeches) cottage

aa. The *Queen's Head*
bb. The United Reformed church
cc. Barrie Parker's vernacular cottages (site of)

45. On 15 November 1733 'John and Jane Phillips surrendered the messuage tenement and yard called the *Raven Inn* now in the possession of Elizabeth Bright being part of a messo known by the name of Brights.'. This building is part of that complex and seems to have been altered many times since it was originally erected.

46. As infilling cut down the area available for livestock markets they moved into more convenient spaces. This photograph of Brook Street (Burway Road) was taken at the turn of the century. The pony fair was held twice a year at the far end of the street.

After the Great Fire

47. (*above*) It is a reasonable assumption that Tudor Cottage was part of the rebuilding after the great fire of 1593. Apart from its unique hewn jetties the house offers a striking example of close studding and decorative framing which were features of buildings of high status. The timbers on the north wall reveal that the roof was raised at some time.

48. (*overleaf*) The rear of Tudor Cottage is in complete contrast to the front. Such timbers as can be seen are in square framing which was used for less important parts of houses. The end of the cross wing bears the date 1779 and, as this is obviously an internal truss and only became an outer wall when one or two bays were dismantled, we presume the date refers to that event.

49. This drawing of a view of the *King's Arms* not usually seen reveals that it is a particularly good close studded building. The stuccoed front conceals further timber-framing. '1760. Thos Mills Shoemaker surrendered the close or yard now divided into 2 peices and parcells of a certain messuage called the Kynges Armes.'

50. It is presumed that this Market Hall (1617), commissioned by Bonham Norton, King's Printer and lord of the manor, was the first, but it may well have replaced an earlier building destroyed in the great fire. Whether it was framed by the legendary John Abel is open to question.

The Old Rectory

51. The Rectory is a late Georgian/early Victorian house which stands on the site of an earlier building and rectors Mainwaring (1749-1807), Coleman (1807-48) and Pemberton (1818-49) were probably all involved in the reconstruction which was obviously never conceived as a complete unit. Until the 1930s a great fig tree grew in the conservatory.

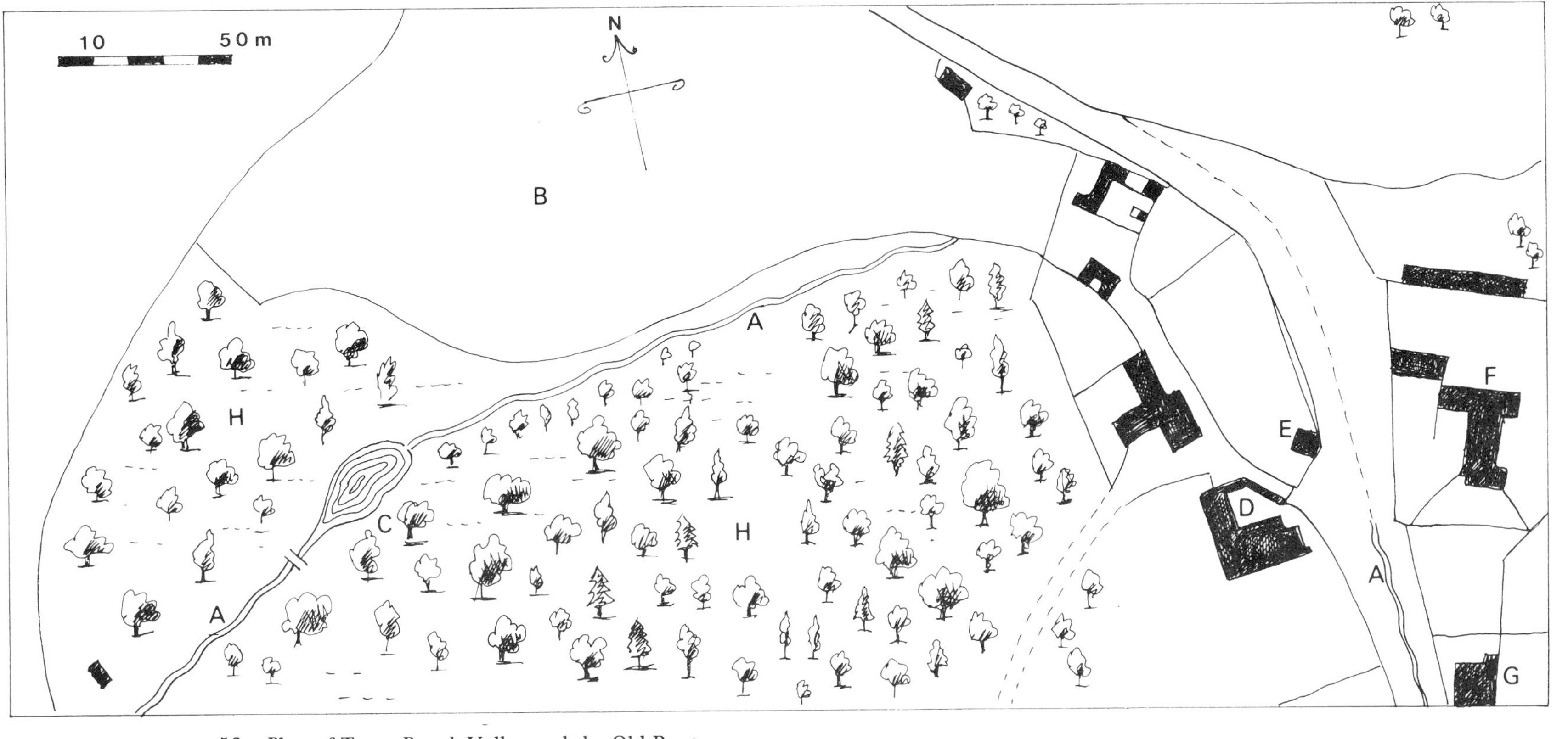

52. Plan of Town Brook Valley and the Old Rectory.
A. The Town Brook, B. Scotchman's Piece, C. The Ice House, D. The Old Rectory, E. Pryll Cottage, F. The Old Bank House, G. The Free School, H. Rectory Woods.

53. (*above*) Trees have obscured much of this side of the house which is dominated by the doric portico at the front door, a feature rarely seen by the public. Had the Rectory been designed as a whole one feels that the main entrance would have been in the centre of the south front.

54. (*left*) The Rectory is now divided into four houses. This main staircase is one of the most elegant features of the interior but a simpler and equally well designed one is to be found in the rear of the building.

68. (*above*) This is the Old Barn as it appeared a few years ago before the Wittings took it in hand. It is a triumph for the conservationists that it survived. The building is a typical 17th-century, three-bay, timber-framed building with square panels, very straight tension braces and Y struts at the gable ends.

69. (*below*) The restored Old Barn is an outstanding example of the use to which old buildings can be put. This is true conservation as the building today is not a fossil but one which not only looks attractive but is also providing a service for the community, as an antique shop.

70. Dr. Mott's home and coach house. Dr. Charles Mott was born in London *c.* 1790. He worked in Rugby, where he met his wife Mary Jane, before coming to Church Stretton about 1819. By all accounts he was a very well-liked member of the community, but the story that the pathway beyond the Carding Mill was named after him is not supported by documentary evidence.

71. No. 47 High Street was originally two cottages occupied in 1841 by Mary Wood, a baker, James Fewtrell, a tailor, and their families—altogether ten adults and four children. The Fewtrells were living there until 1885 at least. The cottages are timber-framed and until quite recently their gardens contributed a lovely oasis of colour to the High Street.

72. The Town Hall, described by Pevsner as being in a 17th-century style, replaced Bonham Norton's excellent timber-framed market hall in 1840. It was declared unsafe and pulled down during the summer of 1963.

73. Henry Wood, ironmonger and the Shrewsbury Old Bank. In 1871 Wood's daughter Clara was fourteen. Wood employed an apprentice, Henry Salt (15), and it seemed that there might be a Dick Whittington situatio However, when the 1881 censu became available it was found that young Salt was no longer mentioned. Henry was a widow and Clara had become his hous keeper.

74. The Salts, who eventually acquired Wood's ironmonger's shop, built the fine Victorian frontage in 1901. Similar buildings were once a feature of our High Streets but so many have been lost that it seems imperative that we conserve the few that remain. The Ruabon brick work is particularly interesting.

75. Scenes like this were commonplace outside game and poultry dealers' premises, particularly at Christmas time. The rods on which the produce was hung were in situ until quite recently. New regulations mean that such displays will never be seen again.

76. Thomas Proffit was first recorded at No. 6 The Square in 1851. He was a draper from Wavertree and Ann, his wife who came from Rochdale, was a confectioner. In 1871 he described himself as a draper and grocer. Ten years later he was still in business and his eldest son had established another shop in the town.

Education

77. A study of the west wall of Burway House (the Free School) reveals the stonework of the earlier building, while plate 82 shows the bell tower. The charity of Thomas Bridgman (1718) 'devised to the school 40 shillings yearly to be paid to the schoolmaster on condition that he should teach four poor children till they could perfectly read the Bible.'.

78. With the opening of the Public Elementary Endowed School in 1861 the old Free School became a private house occupied by Samuel Harley Hough, a solicitor. It subsequently became a private school for boys. Since then it has housed a dentist's surgery and is now divided into flats.

79. The Elementary School served Church Stretton from 1861 until the new primary school was built on the Shrewsbury Road. It was the first example of a neo-timber-frame building to be erected in the town. It now houses the Public Library and Information Centre.

80. Park House, formerly 'the Park', where Elizabeth Shingles started her boarding school for girls after the Corfields had closed their establishment. Subsequently it became the home of Arthur E. de Zrinyi, who according to the 1871 census was an officer in the Austrian army, born in Moldavia. By 1905 he was established and held a variety of public appointments. His widow and daughter carried on a successful welfare clinic at Park House and subsequently at the Silvester Horne Institute.

81. Brockhurst, built on the gravel ridge to the north of the castle site and the only plot which the Stretton Land Company succeeded in selling in that area. For many years it was a preparatory school, taken over by St Dunstan's during the Second World War. It later became a seminary of the Montford Fathers, where students studied philosophy and theology before going abroad. It has now been divided into flats.

The 19th and early 20th Centuries

82. This is a careful copy of a pencil and wash drawing in the vestry of St Laurence's church. It is dated 1852 and on the back are the words 'Probably by a pupil of Philip Vandyck Browne.'. It shows the Town Brook before it was controlled in a conduit and also the bell tower of the Free School.

83. Very few records or pictures of the Union Workhouse have survived. Built in 1838, it was a typical ugly stone building whose object was to discourage paupers and make life as grim as possible for those unlucky enough to seek shelter there. For the old, without means, it was all that was left.

84. This fascinating water colour painted from the railway bridge (dating it after 1852) shows Station Road, formerly Lake Lane and subsequently Sandford Avenue, devoid of buildings, with the town beyond nestling in the shelter of the hills. The field on the left is London Meadow and that on the right is Matthew's Meadow.

85. (*right*) Poster advertising a farmers' and tradesmen's ball, 1862.

86. (*below*) *World's End Inn* formerly the *Grapes* is not mentioned in 1841 but in 1851 Thomas Harley was the innkeeper while his wife, Mary, was a 'carrier to Shrewsbury' and a poulterer. In 1871 George Marsh, the landlord, was also a rural letter carrier and engaged in a variety of activities apart from inn-keeping.

CHURCH STRETTON.

A FARMERS' AND TRADESMEN'S

BALL!

WILL TAKE PLACE

IN THE TOWN HALL,

ON FRIDAY, FEBRUARY 28th, 1862.

PATRONS.

R. WAINWRIGHT, ESQ. | R. MINTON, ESQ.

STEWARDS.

MR. HOGGINS, Botvyle, | MR. G. ROBINSON.
MR. HAYNES, Ragdon, | MR. HENRY BRIDGMAN,
MR. R. MINTON, JUNR. | MR. H. WOOD.
MR. JAMES PHILLIPS.

Ladies' Tickets, 5s. 6d. Gentlemen's Tickets, 7s. 6d.

The favour of your Company and that of your Friends is particularly requested.

Dancing to commence at Nine o'Clock.

MR. SAMUEL LEE COVER'S QUADRILLE BAND, has been engaged for the occasion.

In order that all necessary arrangements may be properly carried out, it is desired that early applications be made for Tickets to the several Stewards.

87. This postcard of a view photographed from the area where the war memorial now stands is undated but the ladies' dresses suggest the end of the 19th century. Part of the Town Brook seems to have been placed in conduit but the church tower has not been given its pyramidal roof.

88. The corner of Back Lane and Cunnery Road. The photograph is dated 1906 though it might well have been taken earlier. In the background is a stonemason's yard and a building which is not shown on the 1838 plan but appears on later O.S. plans. It has since been pulled down, probably when the road was widened.

89. (*above*) The first mention of the exploitation of pure spring water at Stretton was in 1881 when the Church Stretton Aerated Water Co. opened in the Carding Mill Valley using water from the Long Mynd spring. In 1883 the Stretton Hills Mineral Water Company opened a factory next to the Halfway houses on the Shrewsbury Road.

90. (*right*) This factory was eventually taken over by Jewsbury and Brown who ran it successfully for many years. It was one of the principal employers of labour in the town and was known affectionately by local people as the 'Pop Works'! Subsequently the spring and works were acquired by Wells Drinks of Tenbury Wells who bottle and distribute the product throughout the British Isles.

91. By 1850 the *Talbot* had ceased to be the principal ho of the town and that positior had been taken over by the *Crown* which happened to be the nearest inn to the new ra way station. In 1865 the inn extended and renamed the *Hotel*, which meant that an c malthouse had to be pulled down. This stone was incorp ated in the new building.

92. The new hotel was desi in a rather flamboyant Gothi revival style and was much a mired by John Betjeman. Th steps to the main entrance ar particularly interesting. Sinc the fire of 1968 the trade ha been carried on in the old *Cr* premises and the original nar is remembered in the portico designed in the form of a cro

67. High Street looking south. On the right are the *Plough*, the Victorian market hall and beyond, the *Raven*, while on the left is the *Lion* and the Central Boarding House. All the inns are now closed; the *Lion* became Miss Smith's old-fashioned haberdashery shop and is now a newsagents. This drawing shows a less congested High Street than would be seen on market days today.

65. & 66. This was the home of George and Mary Corfield. Mary bore 11 children between her marriage in 1791 and 1812 when Jane, the youngest child was born. George died in 1830. The eldest daughter Ann and three of her sisters, Martha, Elizabeth and Jane, established Ragleth House as a boarding school for girls. This closed sometime after 1851 and in the 1861 census the sisters are described as retired governesses. They were still living at Ragleth House in 1871 but ten years later only Martha (aged 87), who was blind, and Jane were left. The house today has a much altered Georgian front (65 above) with a lovely door (66), while at the rear three quaint Gothick windows can be seen (65 below). Many Strettonians remember the house as Dr. Gooch's surgery.

63. The *Raven* (Bright's Mess age) which was an inn until qui recently. Before the war, when Dennis Williams delivered milk from the farm, he finished his round in the *Raven* yard. Hote and boarding houses insisted o having their milk delivered bef 8 a.m. in time for the guests' breakfasts.

64. The *Brittania* was first me tioned in the 1851 census and this photograph was taken at it closing down sale *c.* 1895. The auctioneer is Mr. Edwards and the lady wearing a bonnet is M Fewtrell. On the left of the auc tioneer is Nancy Wragg, while t child with a daffodil is Maud Roberts.

62. These timber-framed cottages were in what is now the garden of 'Greengates'. They had been covered with stucco, either to disguise their Gothic appearance or for insulation, probably the latter. One was the home of Richard Haughton, the beastleech, and the other in 1841 housed James Bellingham, a hairdresser.

60. The doorway opens into a panelled hall with a dog-leg staircase. From *c.* 184 until 1892 the house was occupied by th Wildings who were surgeons. It was then let to a Dr. Fleming and in 1898 the surviving Wilding, Henry, who was living on the Gold Coast, sold it to Frances Rawlings, who converted it into a boarding house.

61. This photograph of the Central Hotel and Boarding House comes from an advertisement in a local guidebook. It must, judging by the clothing worn by the staff, have been taken early in the present century. The early 18th-century house still has the rightness of proportion of its time.

High Street or Bristol Road

59. The narrowness of the burgage plot forced the builders of No. 17 High Street, previously Berry's Messuage, to place this fine doorway at the side of the house. It is one of several good doorways which have survived in Church Stretton.

57. Pryll Cottage, which is timber framed and subsequently encased in brick, no doubt stood here before the Rectory gardens were laid out. The author believes that the original track to the hills followed the valley of the Town Brook but was rerouted to provide space for a large walled kitchen garden.

58. During the 19th century there was a lodge beside these gates and it was customary for the rector to travel the short distance to church in his horse and carriage. The Old Rectory was eventually sold and a new one erected on Longhills Road; this has recently been turned into an old people's home.

55. To maintain a supply of ice throughout the year the well-to-do built ice houses (sometimes called snow wells). They were sunk in the ground and thatched; superior ones were built of brick or stone and vaulted. Normally they were close to a pond which supplied the ice. The site of this ice house can be traced close to the reservoir in Rectory Woods.

56. This ceiling is in the rear part of the Old Rectory and until recently was covered in plaster. Some of the timbers are obviously from an older building and have been re-used, lending further credence to the suggestion that this was not the first house on the site.

93. As the century progressed the holiday trade increased and in 1899 the *Hotel* was extended down Sandford Avenue. This photograph shows the building just before this happened, with the road beyond devoid of houses or shops. In 1905 a further extension was built along Shrewsbury Road.

94. In 1901 Ralph Beaumont Benson started to sell building plots in Stretton. On 18 June three were offered for sale by auction and No. 22 Sandford Avenue was lot two. It was sold to Thomas Rich, a watchmaker and also the maker of the fine clock which still graces the building. This drawing is based on a postcard *c.* 1907.

95. The Sandford Monument and Coat of Arms. On 19 December 1884, from somewhere close to this monument, a triumphal arch was stretched across to the *Hotel*. From its centre hung a shield bearing the words 'success to the Sandford Avenue'. It was also near here that George Preece, nurseryman and gardener, handed a spade to the Rev. Holland Sandford with which he planted the first tree of his avenue.

96. Gradually Sandford's avenue was developed and by the 1920s there was a post office, banks and numerous shops. Sandford's dream was coming true and his avenue was becoming the most important thoroughfare in the town. Unfortunately a number of his lime trees were already disappearing.

97. (*above*) Little had happened in Back Lane or Church Street for many years apart from the building of the new Public Elementary Endowed School in 1861 on part of Talbot Meadow; then in 1886 an excellent terrace of neo-timber-frame cottages was erected. This drawing shows Nos. 29-37 Church Street.

98. (*right*) Queen Victoria's Diamond Jubilee of 1897 did not go unnoticed in Church Stretton and a terrace of new Ruabon brick houses was named in her honour. A Jubilee fountain was erected beside a small garden where the Midland Bank now stands. It was the building of the latter that caused the fountain to be moved to the top of Brook Street; finally increased traffic caused its disappearance into a Council yard and apparently much of it is now lost.

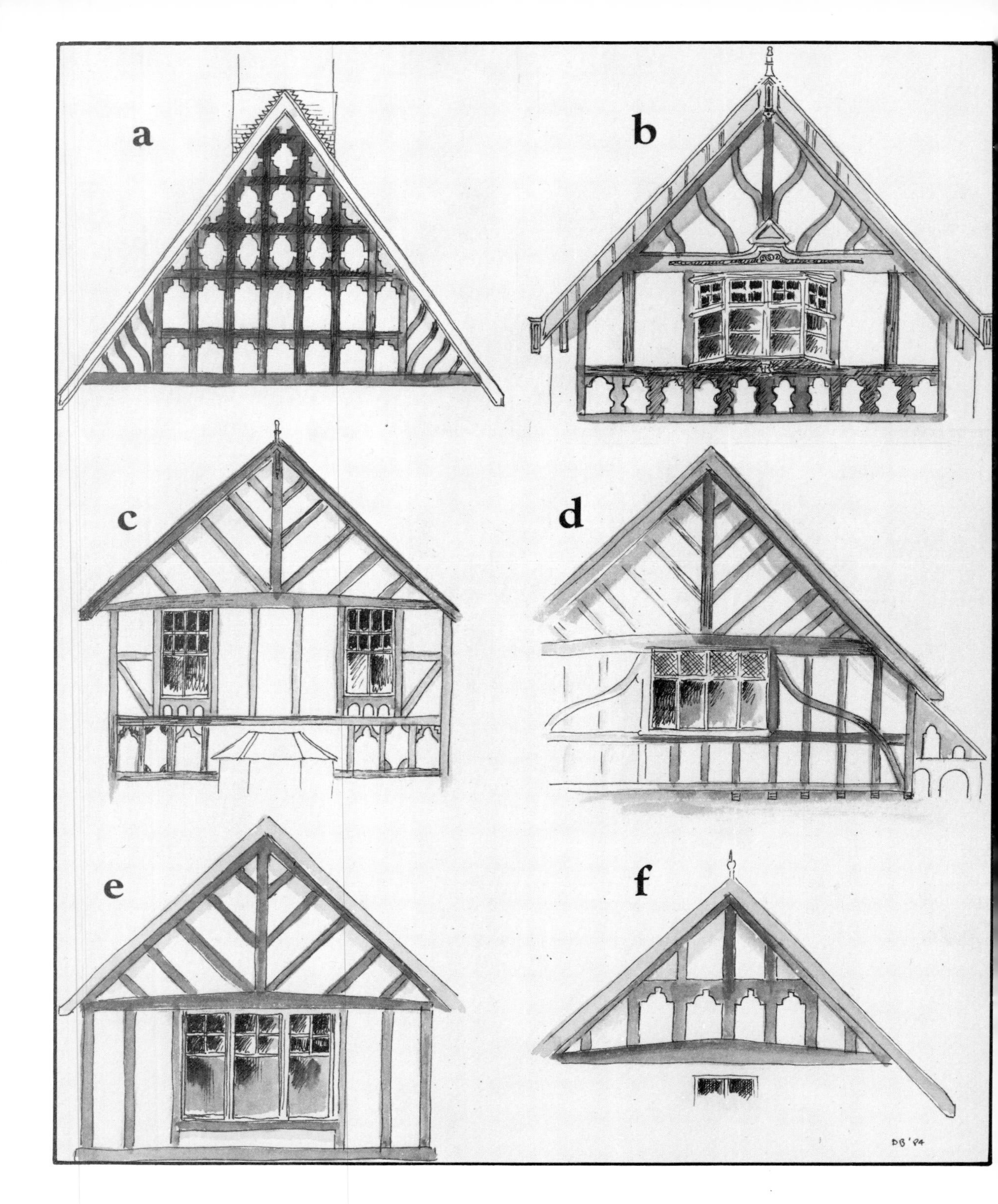
a
b
c
d
e
f
DB '84

99. (*opposite*) Pevsner said that half-timber was the hallmark of Church Stretton, especially of gables. Here are a selection of some of the best: a. 'Overdale', b. Jubilee Buildings, c. 28 Sandford Avenue, d. 'The Rowans', e. 'Colwyn', and f. 'Holmwood'.

100. As the development of the town gathered momentum a power station was built. It had two gas engines, each with 12 ft. flywheels which charged banks of batteries and supplied D.C. electricity to the town. In 1905 it was available at 6d. (2½p.) per unit. It had risen to 1s. (5p.) per unit by 1914.

101. (*above*) The Hydropathic Establishment ('Hydro'). This drawing attempts to portray the *Long Mynd Hotel* as it was originally designed. Unfortunately only photographs taken from a distance seem to have survived. It was built at the height of the neo-timber-frame renaissance in Church Stretton and one feels that it must then have fitted into the landscape far more pleasantly than is the case today.

102. (*below*) This is the second stage in the hotel's development. The fine roof with dormers and much of the character of the building have disappeared. Worse was to come when the view through the Stretton Gap was to be dominated by colossal letters spelling out the name of the hotel.

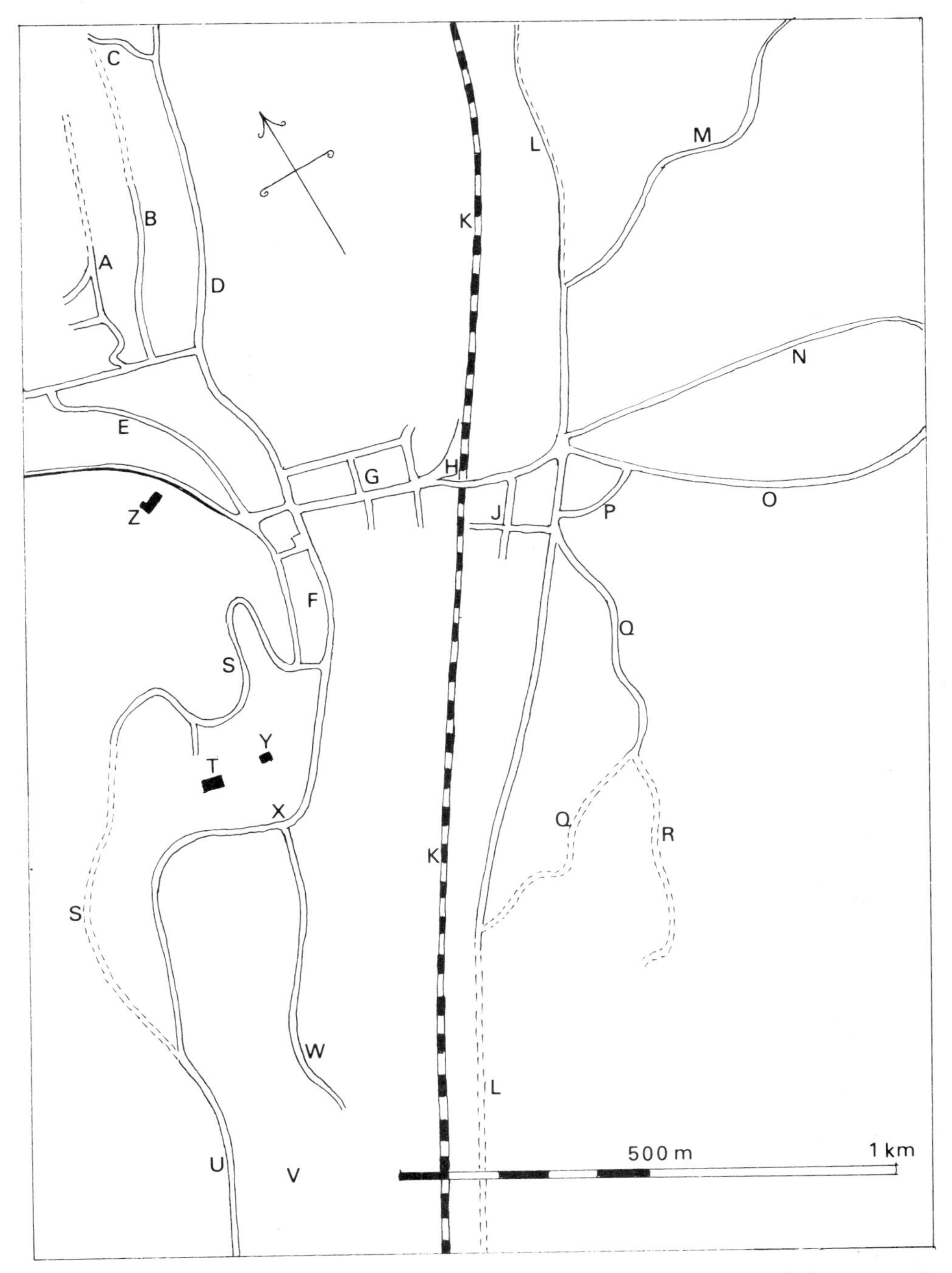

103. Map to illustrate the expansion of Church Stretton *c.* 1890-1910 and the new roads planned and laid out by the Stretton Land Company. Kenyon Road and the extensions to Cunnery Road, Madeira Walk, Trevor Hill and Clive Avenue were never completed. A. Trevor Hill; B. Madeira Walk; C. Cwm Dale; D. Union Workhouse; E. Longhills Road; F. The Medieval Town; G. Sandford Avenue (Stage 1); H. The first Railway Station; J. Crossways; K. The L.N.W. & G. W. Joint Railway; L. Watling Street; M. The Old Cardington Road; N. Sandford Avenue (Stage 2); O. The Old Hazler Road; P. Hazler Crescent; Q. Clive Avenue; R. Kenyon Road; S. Cunnery Road; T. The Hydro; U. The Ludlow Road; V. Brockhurst Castle; W. Brockhurst; X. World's End; Y. Woodcote; Z Scotsman's Field.

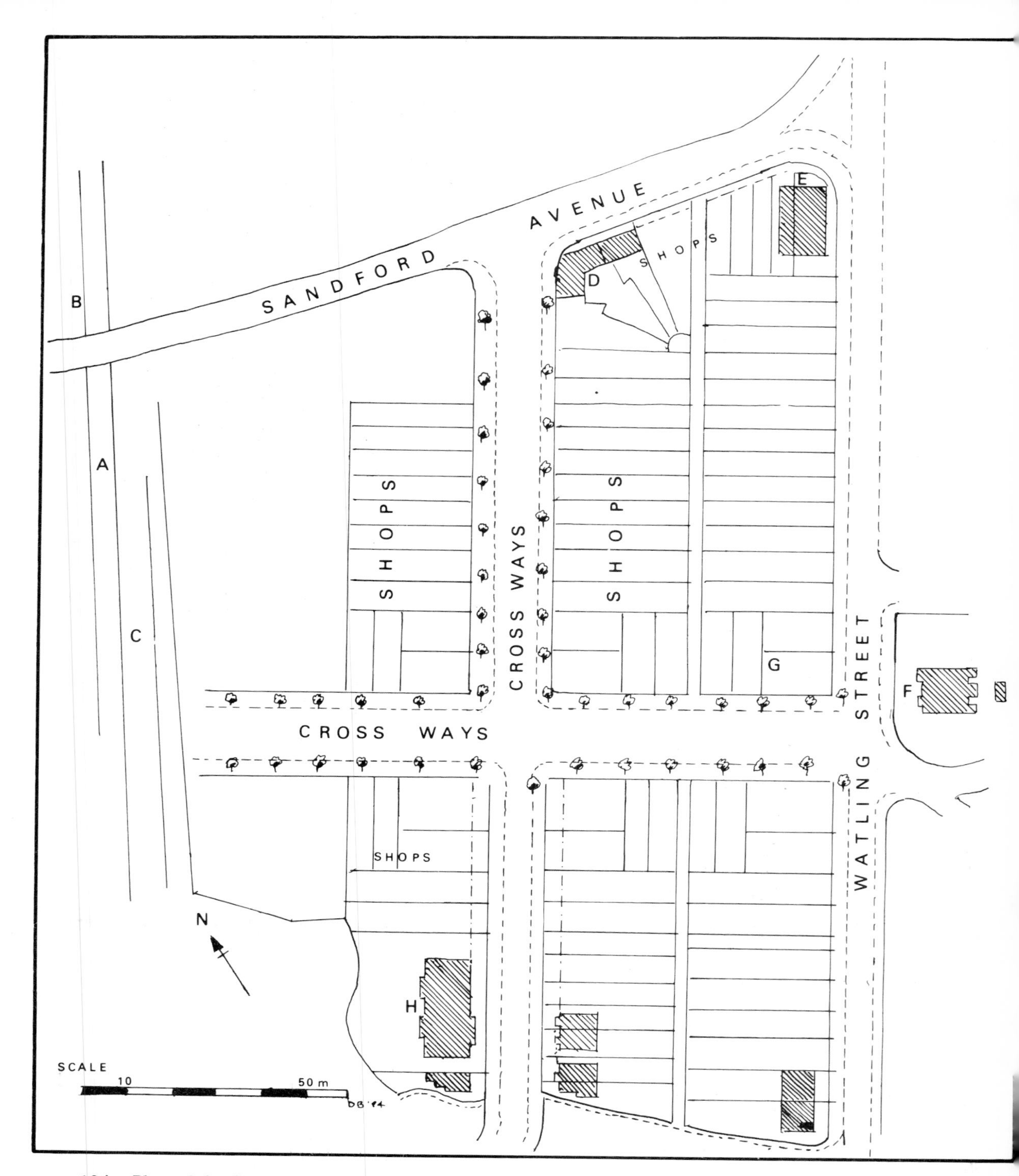

104. Plan of the Crossways Development. This is part of a plan produced by the Stretton Land Company and published with the particulars of a great sale of building plots which took place on 20 July 1905. It suggests that the planners of those days visualised a shift in the position of the town centre to a shopping area adjacent to a new railway station.
A. The L.N.W. & G.W. Joint Railway (Shrewsbury & Hereford); B. The first Railway Station; C. The second Railway Station (finally opened 1913); D. Tower Buildings; E. Vernon House (Wheatley's shop); F. The Sandford; G. The Methodist church; H. The power station.

105. & 106. Exterior and interior views of 'Woodcote'. 'Woodcote' and 'Scotsman's Field' are according to Pevsner 'two especially good houses of the best period of Church Stretton'. Barry Parker, the architect of 'Woodcote', practised in Buxton and eventually went on to draw up the masterplan for Letchworth Garden City. It is one of Parker's most important early houses and was built in 1896 for Campbell Hyslop, owner of the Stretton House Lunatic Asylum for Gentlemen. The original plan envisaged a drive leading to gates and a lodge on the Ludlow Road but no evidence has been found to show that the lodge was ever built.

107. (*above*) 'Scotsman's Field' was designed by Sir Ernest Newton and dates from towards the end of the 'best period'. It is named after the meadow on which it is built, Scotchman's Piece, originally a gathering place for travelling pedlars or hucksters who were called Scotchmen whatever their actual nationality.

108. (*below*) Architects are usually remembered by their larger flamboyant buildings but here, in addition to Barry Parker's 'Woodcote', Church Stretton has two cottages he designed in a vernacular idiom. It is presumed that they were built to house estate servants; in fact, as Cunnery Road was not yet built, they were in a sense lodges to the tradesmen's entrance.

109. Tower Buildings were the first units of the shopping area of Crossways to be completed. In fact, with Wheatleys round the corner, they were the only part of the project ever to get off the drawing board. With the opening of the bypass they became Church Stretton to many motorists using the A49 regularly.

110. Their design is reputedly based on the 'Rows' of Chester and the corner is very similar to Walton's Corner in that city. Church Stretton still mourns their loss; they were pulled down in 1965 because they impeded the view of the motorist, and to make way for a roundabout which was never built.

111. Arden House is an exceptionally good example of neo-timber-frame building. The detail is quite fascinating and worthy of study—the ridge tiles, the porch, doorway, square-cut jambs, windows and leaded lights. The verandah on the right is not original. Like other large houses in the town Arden House is now a private residential home for the elderly.

112. 'The Rowans'. Rowans cottage on the right of the photograph was built on an encroachment of the common and stucco may hide a genuine timber frame. 'The Rowans' itself is another example of the new building which took place at the turn of the century.

113. 'Overdale'. This photograph, taken from the air, suggests that the garden was originally planned to be part of the neo-'Jacobethan' design.

114. This photograph shows the early development of Trevor Hill and the Longhills. Looking at the area today, with houses partly hidden by mature trees, it is hard to imagine that the hillside once looked as scarred as it does in this photograph. The tragedy is that the people who had the courage to build never enjoyed the fruits of their labours.

115. (*left*) Early in the century the malting industry seems to have been rationalised and instead of numerous small malthouses at the top of the town this large one was built at the corner of Easthope Road. It is a superb example of the brickwork of the period and it is probably as important that we list such buildings as we do our older and more picturesque ones. During the war it served as a canteen for the troops and also as workshops for St Dunstan's.

116. (*below*) The expansion of Church Stretton *c.*1907/8. Taken about 1907, this picture shows the expansion of the town to the east of the railway line. Crossways, Hazler Terrace, the Methodist church and Watling Street stand out clearly.

117. Tiger Hall. These large houses occupy the site of an earlier estate cottage and during World War II were used by St Dunstan's as a hospital. A number of Strettonians remember hearing that their parents took part in Miss Auden's great historical pageant which was staged in the natural amphitheatre on the left of this picture. The Auden family was also involved in the work of transcribing Church Stretton's parish registers.

The Railway

118. The first railway station to the north of the road bridge, which is another of Church Stretton's buildings which deserves to be listed. This is one of Mr. Brassey's superb stations on the Shrewsbury-Hereford line. It is built completely in stone from a quarry at Soudley unlike the other stations on the line which only have stonework around the windows.

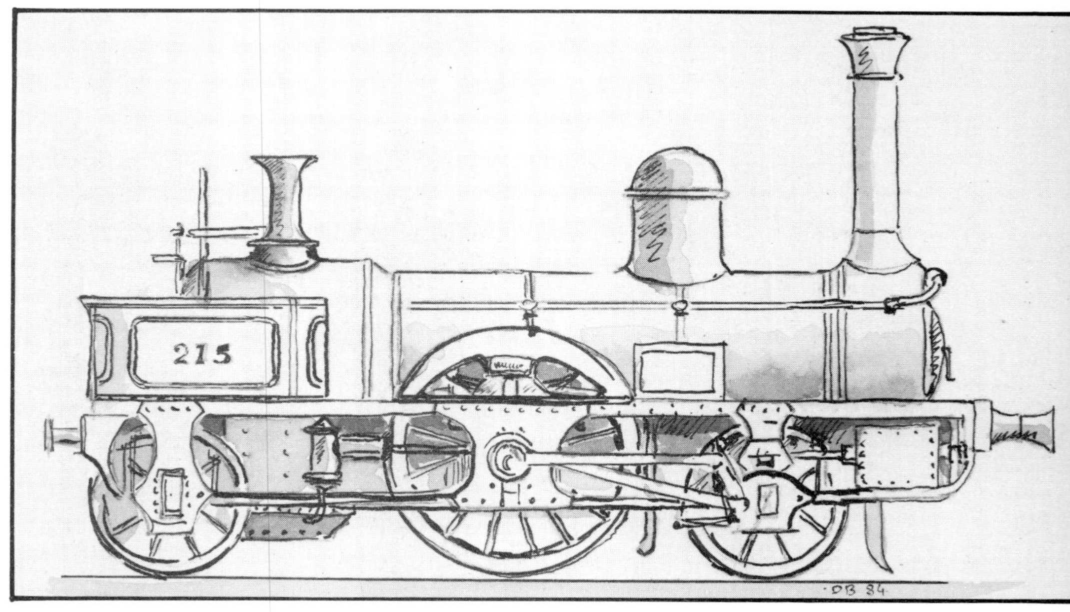

119. One of the locomotives of the Shrewsbury-Hereford line, subsequently transferred to the Great Western.

120. The railway and its sidings, serving a considerable hinterland, were important employers of labour in the town. The terrace at the southern end of Watling Street South is known as the Railway Houses. From a social point of view, it is interesting to note that they are built at the farthest point possible from the town, just as the first council houses were built far away down the Ludlow Road.

121. As promised in the sale literature of 1905, the station did move to the south of the road bridge in 1913 when increasing traffic demanded longer platforms. The fine Railway Gothic buildings have been demolished and the station has been left with 'bus shelter' waiting rooms.

122. The station yard in its heyday. The rows of waggons and heaps of coal served a considerable area around the Strettons. The building on the left is Essex House.

123. Memories of those days when waggons had not only the names of the various railway companies but also a great variety of private owners as well. A goods train, with a brake van of course, provided a geography lesson in itself. This photograph shows the Hyslop waggon.

124. The days of steam are long past but occasionally one rushes to the window as the valley echoes to the shriek of a steam whistle and a white plume of steam billows along the track. Sometimes one happens to be crossing the bridge by the station and can enjoy the distinctive smell. Or the train may stop for a few minutes so that one can stand alongside those giants of our childhood.

Spring Terrace and Brook Street

125. Spring Cottage. The north side of Burway Road was called Spring Terrace in earlier census records and the name has been preserved in No. 8, Spring Cottage. It is an interesting house but its location does not conform to the regular planning of the town. It may be built on a much earlier site.

126. The Church Stretton Posting Establishment was started by the Hyslop family during the latter part of the 19th century. In some towns the blacksmith's shop developed into the local garage, in others as in Stretton, the livery stables. The Central Garage still uses many of the buildings shown in this photograph.

127. Brook Street, now Burway Road. The neo-timber-frame house replaced a row of small cottages, occupied in 1841 by agricultural labourers and by Elijah Price, a weaver. The first post office was on the left, opposite the *Hotel*, and during the 1880s George Windsor was postmaster. In addition to being secretary to Holland Sandford's committee, he also made strenuous efforts to promote the town as a tourist centre.

The Long Mynd

128. Only a few ponies are to be seen on the Long Mynd nowadays. As explained in the introduction, with the demand for pit ponies dying out, fewer were reared on the hills and as a result the ecology of the area has changed considerably, resulting in an increase of bracken and a reduction in whinberries.

129. Bilberries, blaeberries, whortleberries, but here in Shropshire, whinberries; they used to grow in profusion on the hills and moors until the recent changes in the ecology of the area. They were a necessary source of income to the poorer families and children spent their summer holidays picking the fruit. A man called Burke from Wednesbury is reputed to have had a stall on the corner and bought the berries from the pickers; the fruit was used for making dye. The corner referred to is probably where the Midland Bank now stands.

130. Coal brought to the station by rail had to be distributed by horse and cart. Here, it is taking three horses to pull half a ton of coal up the Burway to the 'House on the Hill' or 'Pole Cottage'. The lead horse returned once the steeper part of the route had been covered.

Two World Wars

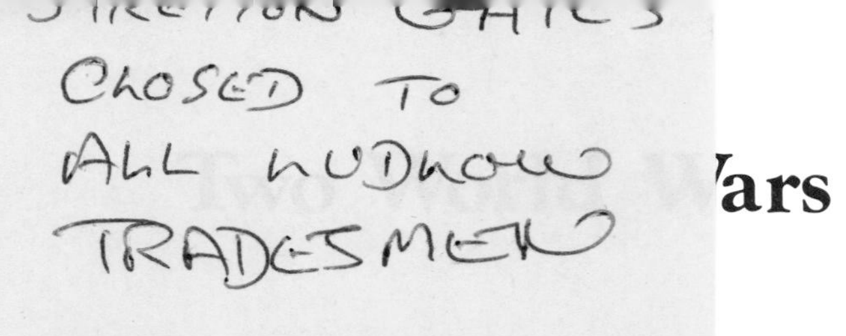

131. (*above*) Helmeth Hill from the railway bridge. Mrs. Poole, whose uncle owned the hill, insisted that two Russians and two landgirls cleared Helmeth of timber during the First World War. It had been previously coppiced. During the Second World War her cousin, Dennis Williams, was attending to a horse over at Gaerstones when two training aircraft crashed in thick fog. One of them tore a track through the trees of Helmeth.

132. (*below*) These lovely iron gates to the park were designed and made by a Flemish refugee called Hermann during the First World War. The park was originally a gift from the Benson family which was added to by the 'Barn Owls', a theatre group which performed in a barn attached to Stretton House. The first moving pictures in Stretton were shown here.

133. (*above*) The Salts, ironmongers of High Street, established their home at 'Highfields' in Sandford Avenue. These buildings were their coach house and stables; they are now Dennis Williams's farm buildings.

134. (*left*) 'Highfields' was taken over by the military during the war and the wooden hut was erected on the front lawn. Beyond, the hen house is built on the foundation of a nissen hut. Dennis Williams also uses nissen huts for his cattle.

CHURCH STRETTON & DISTRICT

WAR WEAPONS WEEK

Aim £20,000.

Programme:

SATURDAY, 24th MAY.

2-45 p.m. "FALL IN" opposite "Tower Buildings."
3-15 p.m. "MARCH PAST" of MILITARY FORCES and ALL SERVICES and "Salute."
3-30 p.m. INAUGURAL SPEECH by Col. G. Windsor Clive, M.P.
7-30 p.m. DANCE in Horne Institute (see special Bills).

SUNDAY. 25th MAY.

2-45 p.m. "FALL IN" for "DRUMHEAD SERVICE," at 3 p.m. to be conducted by the Archdeacon of Ludlow assisted by the Ministers of other Denominations (at the Fountain).

MONDAY, 26th MAY.

2-45 p.m. DISPLAY OF "SCHOOL CHILDREN'S POSTERS" in Cricket Pavilion and Speech by Major-General Tyler.
3-0 p.m. "MILITARY DISPLAY" on Football Field.

TUESDAY, 27th MAY.

5 p.m. to 8 p.m. "ST. DUNSTAN'S LIGHTHEARTED FETE" at the Longmynd Hotel.

WEDNESDAY, 28th MAY.

8-0 p.m. "A VARIETY CONCERT" in the "Silvester Horne Institute" (see special Bills).

THURSDAY, 29th MAY.

Noon. SPEECH by Mr. D. R. Thomas and Cinema Van Speaker at Market.
3-0 p.m. "CINEMA VAN EXHIBITION" at "The Maltings."
3-15 p.m. FOOTBALL MATCH on "Brooksbury Ground."
7-0 p.m. "FULL FIRE AND RESCUE SERVICE DISPLAY" under Police Sergeant Harris, near "[illegible]x House."

FRIDAY, 30th MAY.

2 p.m. to 6 p.m. "WOMEN'S INSTITUTE EXHIBITION," assisted by W.V.S. to be opened by Lady Berwick. *Admission 6d. Stamp.*
7-30 p.m. "A BOY SCOUT CONCERT," also in the Horne Institute. *Admission 1/- & 6d.*

SATURDAY, 31st MAY.

2-45 p.m. MILITARY "PHYSICAL TRAINING" DISPLAY on Football Ground.
3-30 p.m. CRICKET MATCH on "Brooksbury."
8-0 p.m. A DANCE in the Horne Institute (see special Bills).

Announcement of W.W.W. Total here and at "Regal Cinema."

135. A poster publicising War Weapons Week.

136. With the outbreak of the Second World War the military moved into the Stretton area. By 1940, with the enemy just across the channel, St Dunstan's felt that the time had come to leave Ovingdean on the south coast. Church Stretton was away from bombing targets, yet on a main railway line. They moved into the *Long Mynd Hotel.*

137. In his book, *My Story of St Dunstan's* (1961), Ian Fraser writes 'The army told us to keep out' and 'we arrived as gatecrashers'. The move to Church Stretton was piecemeal, starting with the training of First World War men who had recently gone blind and convalescent casualties from the new war. However, within a month or two the hospital also moved to the *Long Mynd Hotel.* Expansion was gradual, huts in the grounds being used as workshops, then the hospital was transferred to Tiger Hall. Separate houses were required for V.A.D.s and teaching staff. Brockhurst was taken over and more huts built in the grounds. This photograph shows a St Dunstan's staff badge.

138. Part of the hotel, Battlefield House and other places were taken over by St Dunstan's and purpose-built workshops for training were erected on the corner of Essex Road and Sandford Avenue. This rather poor picture gives at least some idea of what they were like. After the war the huts housed the Secondary Modern School for a time.

139. The wire and supporting posts by which the men guided themselves can be clearly seen: they were not unique to Church Stretton and the same principle was used at Ovingdean. This photograph shows various VIPs, including the Princess Royal in the centre, visiting St Dunstan's.

Stretton from the Hills

140. Unfortunately the originals of this and the two following engravings have been touched up with water colour. However, they still reveal a considerable amount of witting and unwitting information. One must accept the particularly steep hills as artist's licence. This picture shows Caradoc and Ashbrook.

141. (*above*) The Carding Mill complex. The mill was the building at the rear which has since been pulled down. The mill wheel was on the left and it was powered by water brought by a leet from dams higher up the valley. Traces of the latter feature can still be found today.

142. (*below*) This fascinating picture must have been drawn from the slopes of Ragleth before 1831 because it shows the old timber-frame market hall and the south porch of St Laurence has not been built. There are dormer windows on the Free School and much of Rectory Wood is not planted with trees. The *Talbot* and its associated buildings stand out clearly.

143. If you visit the top car park in Carding Mill Valley you may notice a sign stating that 'the water is three feet deep at this point'. While the sign has remained, the pool, which was used as a swimming pool for many years, has now been filled in. Beyond, up the valley, is Motts Road.

144. World's End and the gas works. On one occasion two visitors arrived in town and put up at one of the inns. They sensed an air of expectancy and on enquiring found out that the new gas lamps were to be lit for the first time. . . The crowds gathered but there was disappointment when one or two lamps flickered only to glow with the light of a penny candle. The townsfolk went home to their beds.

145. View from Clive Avenue *c.* 1906. In the distance are the first buildings on Easthope Road; below, the early development of Watling Street. 'The Brow' on the right was one of the first houses on Clive Avenue. Another, 'The Bungalow' (Hill Cottage), was built for the Chief Constable of the county as a summer residence (1901/9). Their water supply came from a private reservoir on Ragleth.

146. Another of the post-war housing developments—the Stretton Farm Estate built on land formerly attached to Stretton House, Mr. Bakewell's private lunatic asylum for gentlemen. Beyond are Mr. Brassey's railway and the remains of trees planted, one suspects, to hide it. Beyond these are the bypass and the built-up area around Watling Street.

Bringing the Story up-to-date

147. Watling Street Cottage, on the remains of the Roman road. In 1841 it was occupied by Edward Jones, a farmer in a very small way. The expanse of low-lying land beyond the railway had such field names as 'Eel Pool', 'Alder Sough' and 'Marsh'. It is an area whic still floods after heavy rain.

148. Post-war Church Strett has become a retirement area. Several estates have been buil and a large percentage of the houses are occupied by older people. This is Battlefield Estate photographed from th other side of the valley.

149. The early 1980s has seen a move away from the neo-Georgian to neo-Gothic styles of building, and Church Stretton seems to be passing through a mini-neo-timber-frame renaissance. This house (*c.*1984) is part of a small development in the Old Rectory gardens, the site, in all probability, of the original Saxon township.

And beyond Church Stretton lies the parish……

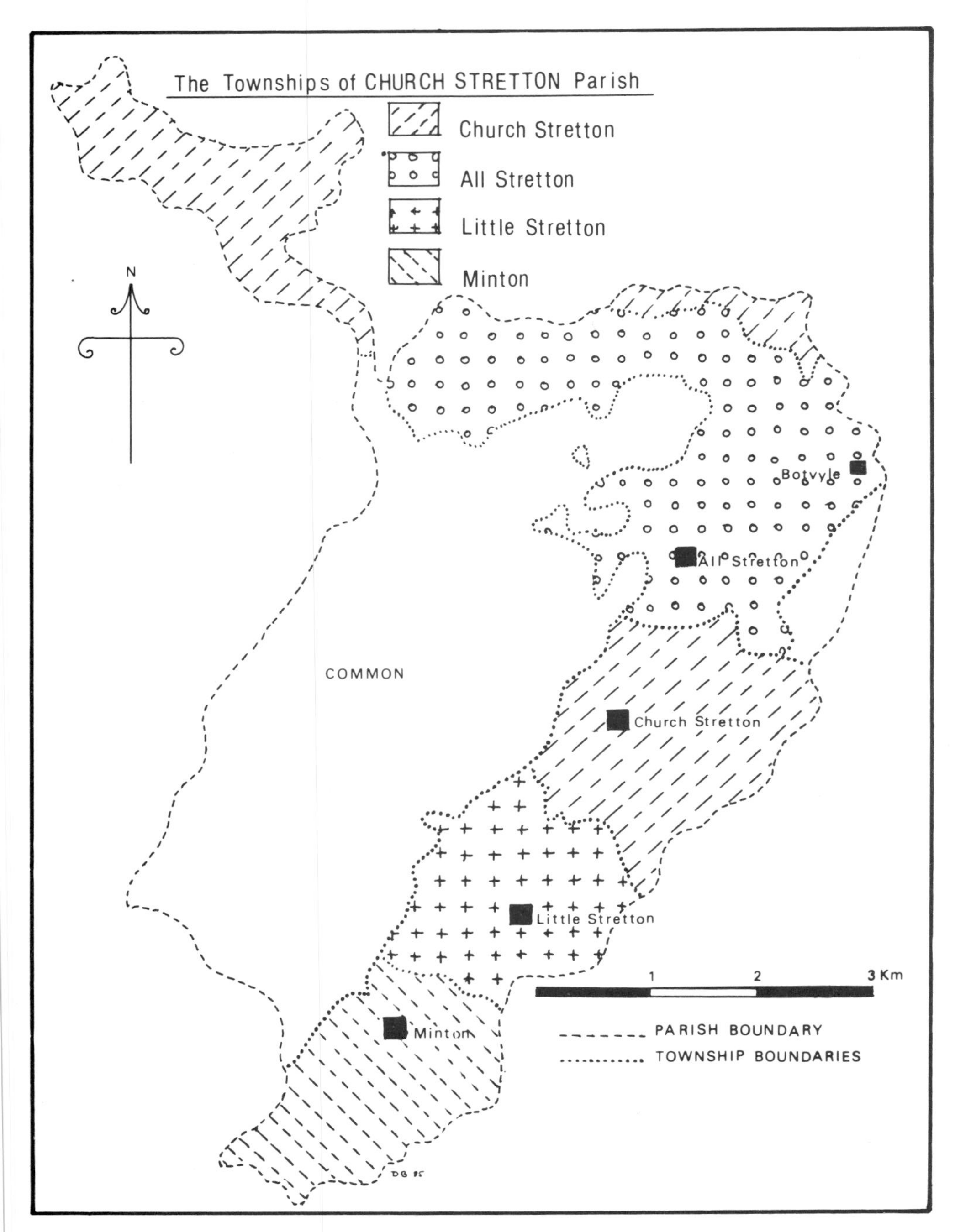

150. Church Stietton is the major settlement in the manor and parish. The Domesday survey states that there were four berewicks in the manor of Stretune. In all probability they were Alured (All) Stretton, Parva (Little) Stretton, Minton and Whittingslow. The latter township is now in the parish of Wistanstow, while Botvyle, once part of Cardington manor, is in Stretton.

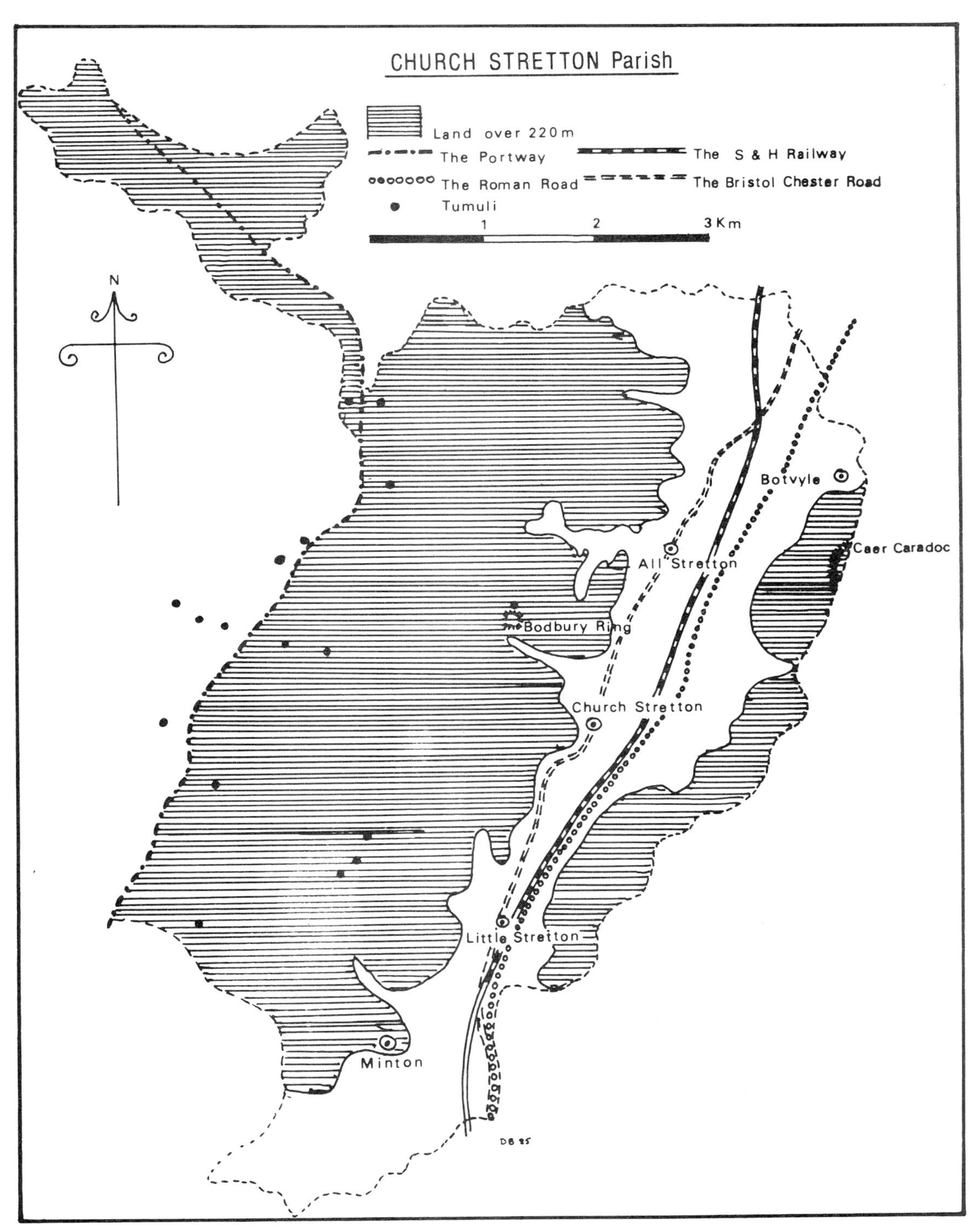

151. This relief map emphasises the importance of the Stretton Gap as a route from north to south but it also shows that before the forests were cleared, the Portway was the principal road. It was used by Neolithic axe traders and was, in fact, still recognised as a King's Highway as late as the Middle Ages. The tumuli are a visible survival of the Bronze Age.

Minton

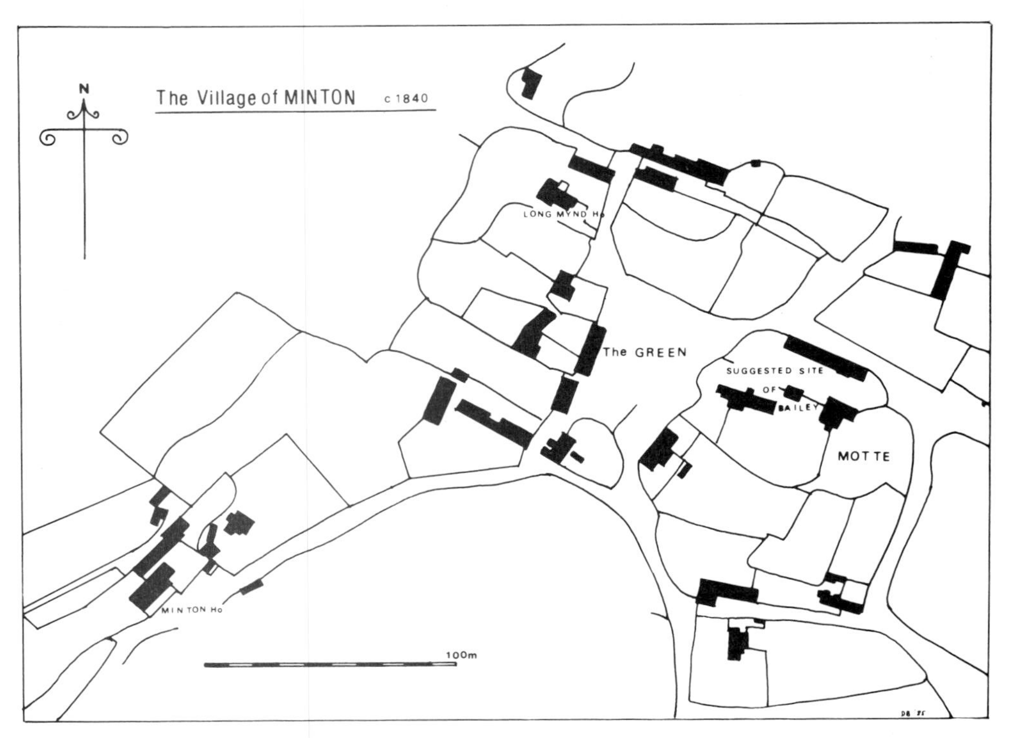

152. Domesday records that the Saxon Earl Leuric held the manors of Munetune (Minton) and Witecheslawe (Whittingslow) but in 1086 they are recorded as being part of the Earl of Montgomery's manor of Stretune. Munetune means the township by the mountain, i.e. the Long Mynd. Pevsner suggests that the cottages and farms around the village green are a typical Saxon arrangement while Rowley feels that the green may have resulted from a remodelling of the settlement when the motte was built by the Normans. The present property boundaries suggest the existence of a bailey running W.N.W. from the motte to the village green.

153. The motte at Minton. This is a small motte which is quite well preserved apart from a lateral trench up the east side. It has a base diameter of about 25 metres, its height is 4.7 metres and its flat summit is 10 metres across. Remains of a ditch are visible.

154. Long Mynd House. An old photograph shows that the crucks on the external wall originally went down to the ground as one would expect. Internally one full cruck is visible and there is also a smoke blackened truss—proof that part of the building was an open hall. The stack and first floor are later insertions. Madge Moran thinks that it may have been a long house and that the byre at the lower end has now disappeared.

155. Minton House. It has been suggested that this was a drovers' inn but so far no documentary evidence has been found to substantiate the claim. The colossal chimney stack projecting from the gable reveals that a much earlier house lurks beneath the Georgian front which is dated 1757. The interior is very fine, particularly the splendid framed newel staircase.

Little Stretton

156. Parva (Little) Stretton is a charming village with a wealth of exposed timber framing. One of the toll gates on the Ludlow-Shrewsbury turnpike stood on a corner close to the church.

157. The church of All Saints was built as a chapel of ease in 1903. It was sent from Manchester by a firm specialising in iron and wooden buildings which could be erected by local builders. The thatched roof was a later improvement paid for by Derwent Wood. It was he, to quote Pevsner, who 'flamboyantly restored and enriched the Tanhouse during the time he lived there.'.

158. The Malt House is a genuine box frame building (*c.* 1500) with 17th-century additions. It was originally an open hall but a floor has been inserted and the roof raised. There are large curved braces on the crosswing and wooden drip moulds to the windows. In the gable is an ulenlock and there are also scotch marks, survivals of the construction technique which involved the erection of the frames on the ground prior to their being raised into position. The barn with its unusual vertical weatherboarding has been pulled down.

All Stretton

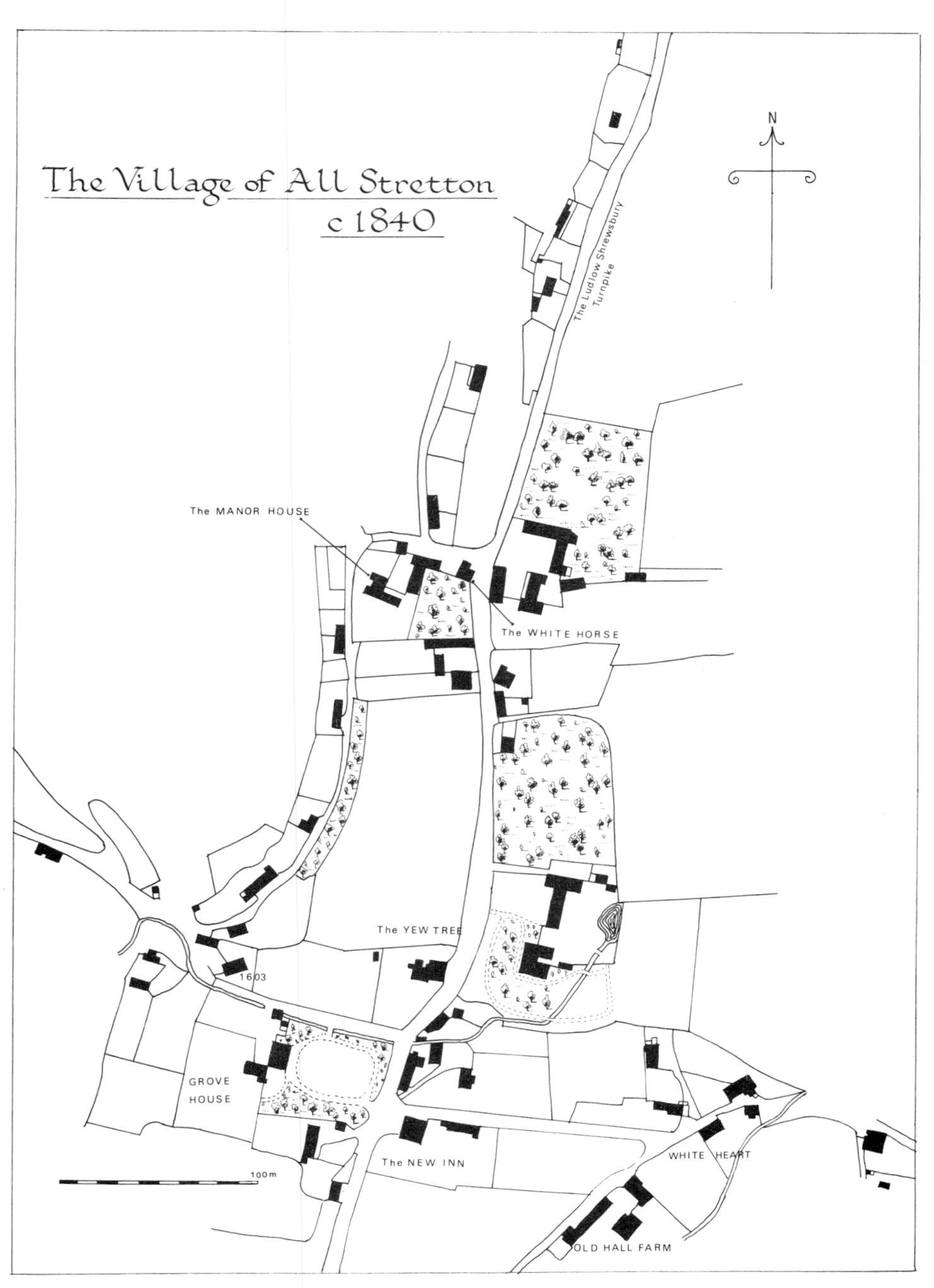

159. Most places have their charming traditional stories of the past and Stretton is no exception. The story of the last stand of Caractacus has already been mentioned and another concerns James I (or sometimes it is James II or even John!) who was journeying from Ludlow to Shrewsbury. As the party approached Little Stretton he inquired its name. 'Stretton, Sire' was the reply. Arriving at Church Stretton the king made the same inquiry and 'Stretton, Sire' was again the reply. Coming to the third township he repeated his question and received the same answer. 'Upon my word' said the king, 'they are all Stretton in this county.' Actually medieval documents name the village as Alured Stretton.

160. In 1838 Grove House was let to William Craig, a schoolmaster. He had six children of his own and in addition ran a boarding school for 13 boys between the ages of 11 and 16. In 1861 it was a Ladies' Private Lunatic Asylum owned by Samuel Bakewell of Stretton House and the census lists Anne Wainwright as matron-in-charge. After Samuel's death Harriet, his widow, was the proprietor. Her neice Hannah married Dr. John McClintock, who had taken over Dr. Mott's practice in Stretton and in 1881 he was proprietor of the Grove, while Harriet lived at Lower House. After John's early death his widow carried on until her son was able to take over the work. The house has been pulled down and the grounds used for a housing estate.

161. As a boy I remember seeing a film in which vagrants and paupers slept standing up with their arms supported by ropes slung across the room. They were woken up when the lodging house keeper untied one end of the rope. I never thought that there was any truth in the story but, apparently, when this building was a licensed lodging house, Dr. McClintock was called in and was amazed to find this system in operation. This drawing is made from an old photograph taken before the building was heavily restored and given the name 'Manor House'. In the past it must have been a particularly fine timber-frame homestead with a very interesting jetty.

162. Old Hall Farm. From the outside this building is something of an enigma, though the position of the door and stack do suggest that the latter has been inserted in an older house. Over the centuries the land has risen at the west side which destroys the proportions somewhat; nevertheless the timbering and the construction of the jetty are worthy of careful study.

163. Built as a chapel of ease in 1902, the church of St Michael and All Angels, All Stretton, is now almost completely hidden by trees. In drawing this picture the author was helped by a small photograph in an old guide book which had been taken when the church was being built and before the steps in the porch and the mock-timber framing had been completed. The architect was Lloyd Oswell.

164. & 165. The Congregational church in Church Stretton extended its meetings to All Stretton in 1872, and until 1895 these were held in this small cottage known as '1603'. They then moved to larger premises in the Old Room a little way up the lane, where services were held until the new mission church was built in 1907. The picture above is from an old drawing of '1603' and the one below shows the building as it appears today with plaster removed from the end wall to reveal substantial timber framing.

166. The *Yew Tree*. The original house was a 17th-century box-framed structure which has been considerably added to, particularly in 1720 when major alterations were made. It was already a hostelry early in the 19th century.

Botvyle

167. A third traditional story concerns a family called Botvile or Bottefelde which was supposed to take its name from the township of Botvyle. During the reign of Edward IV a John Botvile resided at one of the inns of court and acquired the nickname John of th'inne and thus evolved the surname Thynne. This family bought the Augustinian priory of Longleat after the Dissolution of the Monasteries and between 1567 and 1579 built one of the finest Elizabethan houses in England on the site of the priory. The Thynnes who acquired the titles of Viscount Weymouth and later Marquis of Bath, were lords of the manor of Stretton from the late 16th to the early 19th centuries. The picture shows Botvyle Farm before the crosswing was pulled down, and legend has it that a Thynne was living here while Longleat was being built! The west front of the house was replaced with a Georgian front after a fire.

168. This drawing is of the rear of the crosswing. Recent studies suggest the presence of a former road system and house platforms in the orchard south-west of the farm, so Botvyle may be a shrunken settlement. More recently there was coal mining in the area and there are field names such as Coalpit Piece and Coalpit Meadow shown on the tithe map.

169. This building at Lower Botvyle may be the tithe barn.

170. There were at least three mills in the parish, Queenbatch in the south, Dagers or Dudgley in All Stretton and the third in Carding Mill Valley which has already been mentioned. This more detailed drawing shows the latter mill *c.* 1880. It was originally a corn mill but changed functions with Dagers early in the 19th century when it became a carding mill. In 1824 a new three-storey building was added, hand looms and spinning jennies were installed and the owner was described as a wool stapler and flannel manufacturer.

171. Buildings constantly change their function. Here are six which have all, at one time, been alehouses or inns. In All Stretton, a. the *New Inn* is now a private house as is b. the *White Horse* and c. White Heart Cottage which became the *White Heart* for a short time, one of five public houses open during the period in which the railway was being built. The *Lion* in Church Stretton, d., is now a newsagents, and e. is the *Queen's Head.* Finally, f. is the village store in Little Stretton which was once the *Crown.*

Some 15,000 words and 120 pages or more ago I suggested that Church Stretton was a shy place which hid itself away. The same is true of the whole of Strettondale where a remarkable number of good timber-framed buildings have been preserved for posterity. Let us hope that this policy continues and that they continue to remain in the hands of sympathetic owners.

SELECT BIBLIOGRAPHY

Barley, M. W., *The English Farmhouse and Cottage* (1972).
Beck, K. M., *The West Midland lines of the Great Western Railway.*
Beresford, M., *New Towns of the Middle Ages* (1968).
Bilbey, David, Various pamphlets about Church Stretton published by the Stretton Society and by Wells Drinks (1981-5).
Brunskill, R. W., *Illustrated History of Vernacular Architecture* (1971).
Church Stretton: Minutes of the Meetings of the Committee invited by the Rev. Holland Sandford of Eaton to assist in the work of forming an avenue of Limes from the Railway Station to the Hotel Church Stretton (1884-5).
Clifton-Taylor, Alec, *The pattern of English Building* (1983).
Cranage, D. H. S., *An Architectural Account of the Churches of Shropshire (1894-1912).*
Church Stretton Congregational Church (A Short History published for its centenary), (1960).
Cunnington, Pamela, *How old is your House?* (1980).
Ellis, Hamilton, *British Railway History* (1959).
Eyton, R. W., *The Antiquities of Shropshire (1854-60).*
Foxall, H. D. G., *Shropshire Field Names* (1980).
Girouard, Mark, *Life in the English Country House* (1978).
Greig, D. C., *Geology of the Country around Church Stretton, Craven Arms, Wenlock Edge and Brown Clee* (1968).
Harris, Richard, *Discovering Timber Framed Buildings* (1978).
Hewett, C. A., *English Historic Carpentry* (1980).
Hoskins, W. G., *English Landscapes* (1973).
Parry Jones, W. L., *The Trade in Lunacy* (1972).
Lonsdale, Lord Fraser of, *My Story of St. Dunstan's* (1961).
Millward, Roy, and Robinson, Adrian, *The Welsh Borders* (1978); *The Welsh Marches* (1971).
Pevsner, N., *The Buildings of England: Shropshire* (1958).
Phillips, *The Volunteer Army and Church Stretton.*
Platt, Colin, *The Parish Churches of Medieval England* (1981).
Rowley, Trevor, *The Shropshire Landscape* (1972).
Scott, *The Great Great Western* (1903).
Shropshire Libraries, *The Strettons. Scenes from the past* (1979).
Shropshire Parish Registers, Hereford Diocese, Vol. 8.
Stanford, S. C., *Archaeology in the Welsh Marches* (1980).
Taylor, Christopher, *Fields in the English Landscape* (1975).
Trinder, Barrie, *A History of Shropshire* (1983).
Whateley, Rosaleen, *Old Houses in All Stretton*, parts 1 & 2 (1976/7).
Wright, *Geology of the Church Stretton Area* (1968).

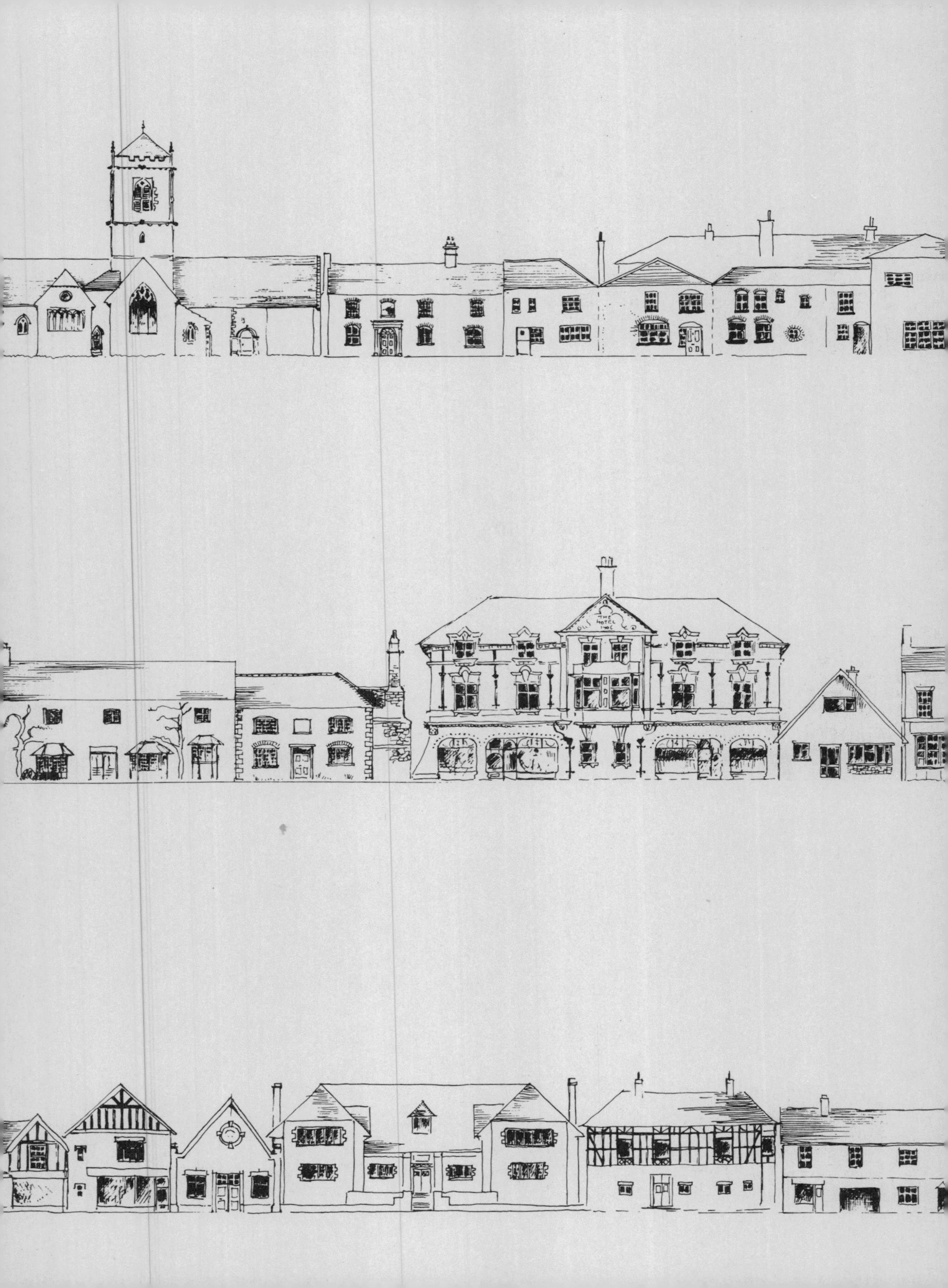
THE
HOTEL